# The Dynamics of Forgiveness

## CECIL BARHAM

### Stopping the Hurts of Offenses from Stopping You

**DYNAMIC:**
**FULL OF LIFE, ACTIVE, MOVING, WORKING**
Dynamic from Greek *dynamikos* meaning Powerful;
Manifesting Continuous Productive Activity and Change.

**FORGIVE:**
**TO RELEASE SOMEONE FROM THEIR INDEBTEDNESS**
To Cease to Feel Resentment Against (an Offender);
To Give Up Resentment of or a Claim to Requital (for an Insult);
To Grant Relief from Payment (of a Debt)
Greek: to send forth, send away; to bestow favor unconditionally

**TIMELY TRUTH MINISTRIES**
Cecil Barham
E-mail: timelytruths@yahoo.com

ISBN: 1482311623
ISBN 13: 9781482311624

Library of Congress Control Number: 2013902020
CreateSpace Independent Publishing Platform
North Charleston, South Carolina

Printed in the United States of America

I DEDICATE THIS BOOK TO MY FAMILY

To my wife,
Darlene Barham

To my three sons and their wives,
Cecil S. Barham
David O. Barham
Aaron B. Barham

To my Grand-Children, my Great-Grandchildren,
And to the Coming Generations

**AUTHOR'S NOTE:** I have endeavored to write this book in a format that will serve the casual reader who desires to get to the matter without the distraction of extra notes and references while still serving the more studious reader as well.

To be sure the full message and its Biblical foundation is presented I include in addition to the Scriptures quoted numerous Scripture references in the main text by printing them in a different and smaller italic type *(illustrated here)* that, while hopefully not being a hindrance to the casual reader, will still serve the reader who is interested in a fuller Biblical background and related truths.

Following each section I have included **Thoughts** with additional insights and Questions for review. At the end of the book is an **Appendix** with brief articles that pertain to a Christian world view.

Then the book contains **sub-headings** to break up the amount of reading material so it can be read in a snack form rather than a large main meal. I know the time squeeze we are all in today.

There are numerous places in which I have placed words of Scripture *in italics* or smaller print with a different font to distinguish them in the text of *The Dynamics of Forgiveness*. In other instances I have made words **bold**, or all CAPITALS, or <u>underlined</u> them for emphasis, or for teaching purposes insert noted thoughts in the Biblical translation form and style itself.

I sincerely hope the format serves everyone well.

*Use of the 1601 KING JAMES VERSION is indicated by (KJV).*

*Use of THE NEW KING JAMES VERSION is indicated by (NKJV).*

*Use of the NEW AMERICAN STANDARD VERSION is indicated by (NASB95).*

*Use of the AMPLIFIED BIBLE is indicated by (Amplified Bible).*

*Use of the Holy Bible, New Living Translation is indicated by (NLT).*

*Use of The Living Bible is indicated by (TLB).*

*Use of the NEW INTERNATIONAL VERSION is indicated by (NIV).*

*Use of THE MESSAGE is indicated by (The Message).*

**DEAR READER:**

Do you have questions about, or, are you unfamiliar with the traditional and historical Judaea/Christian world-view of life?

If so, I recommend first going to the **Appendix** at the back of the book and reading my four short articles on *Taste and See, What Is the Bible?, What Is the Church?*, and *The Biblical Back-Ground of Some Words and Phrases* before reading the main work that starts with Section One, The Impossibility of Offenses.

This book is written with a firm belief in the Bible as the Word of God for the simple reason **it truly works** in a person's day to day life and living. The Bible reveals God's will to all His creation and, especially, to all those who in faith embrace God's Son, Jesus Christ.

God's desire and willingness to wonderfully transform and powerfully work in lives throughout man's history has been and continues to be experienced by many countless millions of people.

It comes as no surprise that there have always been, without pause, people in various places throughout all recorded history who have displayed a belief in God and eternal life.

Where does that undying spiritual stirring come from? From God Himself! When He created us He put this eternal awareness into our hearts.

"He has made everything beautiful in its time. He also has planted eternity in men's hearts and minds [a divinely implanted sense of a purpose working through the ages which nothing under the sun but God alone can satisfy]..." *(Ecclesiastes 3:11 Amplified Bible)*

Remember, there must be and has always been something because it is impossible that there could be nothing. And that something was Some One—God!

Just as a watch with its design, parts, and pieces involving complex working intricacies did not come from an explosion in a field somewhere so man and his world, which are far, far more complex than the finest watches made did not come from a fluke cosmic explosion.

This book is about what this God, Who designed and made us, will do when you truly forgive others who have hurt and offended you so you can stop the deep hurts of offenses that may be stopping you.

# THE BEGINNING OF THE JOURNEY

I have never experienced seeing angels, hearing audible voices, being taken to heaven, or similar experiences as some attest they have. But I definitely experienced something unique from God one Saturday morning when certain truths on what I now call *The Dynamics of Forgiveness* began to unexpectedly pour into my heart.

In this book I share those life-changing truths that came suddenly to me on that Saturday a number of years ago now. This newer, updated, and revised book edition is about those same truths that changed my life and have changed the lives of many, many others that I have shared them with through my first book, pastorates, seminars, and special services. These truths continue proving to be just as relevant today as they were when I first encountered them.

In 1975 I had just come through three of the most challenging years of my entire life up to that point in time. In the midst of God working very effectively in my life and ministry at our pastorate in Northridge, California which was regularly experiencing overflow attendances I was also going through times of feeling deeply betrayed, maligned, attacked, wounded, and greatly hurt.

But even still, in the midst of all this, there was a hunger crying out in my heart to see a mighty work of God done in and through my ministry.

It was during this time that I awoke one Saturday morning on a Thanksgiving holiday week-end and was getting ready for breakfast. I had enjoyed a very pleasant evening of rest. There were no great contemplations, broodings, or such filling my mind. It was just the beginning of the Thanksgiving, Christmas, and New Year holiday season that I have always loved and enjoyed—and still do.

I had been up only a short time when it happened.

Suddenly something (as in Someone) touched my heart and mind. Inwardly I saw the turmoil and turbulence of people and homes in our pastorate. Then that of churches throughout our nation, followed by countless numbers of other homes, families, marriages, and lives.

Immediately following this I began sensing the overwhelming desperation in these lives that had been deeply offended and hurt by what people and life had done to them. Then quickly this was followed by God's answer to their seemingly hopeless struggles and frustrations against the offenses that were crushing them.

God's answer to these relationships torn by offenses and the deep hurt in churches, homes, families, marriages, life, situations, and other instances that I was seeing as hopeless was FORGIVENESS.

Then certain aspects and dynamics of forgiveness began to unfold before me as though I was watching a drama enacted. Things that I did not remember reading or hearing about in some key areas of forgiveness began filling my heart and mind.

A new and exciting journey began that day. I began writing down the thoughts and truths that were breathing with life in me until I had filled many pages with notes.

The next day, which was a Sunday, I shared briefly with the church congregation a little of what had happened the morning before. I did not say anymore, but for the next few weeks I began and continued pouring over many Scriptures related to forgiveness.

I felt restrained by the Lord from bringing any of these truths in a message form until I had probed their meaning and made application of them to my own life.

Torn relationships that had come through offenses in my life must be healed. Things, people, and incidents that had happened not only recently, but years before had to be brought into subjection to this and like areas that is often referred to in Scriptures as a "thus says the LORD" and what is "right in the sight of the LORD".

As I began applying these principles and dynamics of forgiveness to my life, unusual and unique things began to take place. Unpleasant and painful situations of offense began changing. Painful memories began to heal. Heartbreaks mended. People with whom there was a wall of ill-feelings that I had not seen in varying lengths of time began to suddenly contact me. They had changed. Or was it me? Or was it both?

In January of 1976 I began to bring these truths on forgiveness in a series of six messages to our pastorate. Amazing transformations of grace began happening in people's lives. Testimonies started coming in of unexpected restorations and healings in torn relationships that had seemed beyond hope.

Since that time years ago when these Scriptural dynamics and principles of forgiveness were birthed in my heart and spirit I have sought to earnestly live by them in my walk with the Lord, my marriage, my home, and ministry.

These timely truths continue to bring and maintain such a freedom in my life and help me to remain steadfast in the Lord in the face of the ongoing offensive things that still happen and are unavoidable in all of our lives in day-to-day living.

I never planned to write a book or put these messages in printed form apart from my own sermon notes. The first book came about as the results of the encouragement and deep conviction of Everett Smith, who, because of these messages of forgiveness experienced a powerful life-change and became a special friend in Christ to me.

I have since sold and distributed several thousand copies of the original book, preached these messages in many gatherings, received numerous unsolicited testimonies, had the book and its vital truths used in classes of various church denominations and fellowships plus other ministers have used and preached the messages to great effect.

I have received requests to have it translated into Spanish, and still have ongoing inquiries up to this present time about obtaining a copy of the book (either as a first-time purchase or to replace a book given out and circulated among others).

During my most recent pastorate I was approached by a small-group ministry that is both national and international in scope asking that I write a special small-group book on these truths and a study guide for use and distribution by them.

I am still humbled at how this book with its truths on the spiritual dynamics of forgiveness as it is read, taught, and preached remains so relevant, up-to-date, and life changing in so many hearts and lives—even after close to four decades have passed since these truths were first imparted to my heart.

I am convinced from the many testimonies we have received from those that have embraced these truths for their lives that as you read this book and apply the forgiveness dynamics that transformations will take place in your life. There are situations that look seemingly hopeless that are going to change. New vitality in many areas of your life is coming.

As you read and follow these truths do not be surprised by what the Holy Spirit starts doing in your thinking. Let Him do His work. Listen to Him. Follow His directions. Submit to his authority. The Scriptures and the Lord Jesus Christ are going to become a fresh and new life-changing reality in you.

A final thought concerning books overall. There are various reasons why books are written and the ways they are read.

You can read for the sheer pleasure that comes from a well-written book with a well-developed plot that is thoroughly prepared by a person gifted with great literary ability. Or, you may search for understanding in various areas communicated by those gifted in writing who are experienced and knowledgeable in their field.

I make no claims as an experienced and gifted writer or as a great theologian. To be sure a book well written by a person of literary ability and keen knowledge is a bonus to read. However, it may not necessarily be any more or less truth.

This book is not a masterpiece. It is a message. While reading it if you find a bone or two just spit the bones out and enjoy the fish. God bless you as you read!

*Cecil Barham — September 2013*

# TABLE OF CONTENTS

# SECTION ONE

---

# THE IMPOSSIBILITY OF OFFENSES AND THE ULTIMATE OF FORGIVENESS

---

THE UNAVOIDABLE PROBLEM OF OFFENSES

THE TWO BASIC KINDS OF OFFENSES

THE PARTIAL KNOWLEDGE PROBLEM

THREE STEPS IN DEALING WITH OFFENSES

BINDING AND LOOSING

# MATTHEW 18.1–35 *(NKJV)*

## WHO THE GREATEST IN THE KINGDOM ARE

¹ At that time the disciples came to Jesus, saying, "Who then is greatest in the kingdom of heaven?"
² Then Jesus called a little child to Him, set him in the midst of them,
³ and said, "Assuredly, I say to you, unless you are **converted** and **become as** little children, you will by no means enter the kingdom of heaven.
⁴ "Therefore whoever humbles himself as this little child is the greatest in the kingdom of heaven.
⁵ "Whoever receives one little child like this in My name receives Me.
⁶ "But whoever causes one of these little ones who believe in Me to sin, it would be better for him if a millstone were hung around his neck, and he were drowned in the depth of the sea.

## SOLEMN FACT AND WARNING ABOUT OFFENSES IN LIFE

⁷ "**Woe to the world because of offenses!** For **offenses must come**, but woe to that man by whom the offense comes!
⁸ "If your hand or foot causes you to sin, cut it off and cast *it* from you. It is better for you to enter into life lame or maimed, rather than having two hands or two feet, to be cast into the everlasting fire.
⁹ "And if your eye causes you to sin, pluck it out and cast *it* from you. It is better for you to enter into life with one eye, rather than having two eyes, to be cast into hell fire.
¹⁰ "Take heed that you do not despise one of these little ones, for I say to you that in heaven their angels always see the face of My Father who is in heaven.

## GOD'S NATURE AND DESIRE TO SAVE

¹¹ "For the Son of Man has come to save that which was lost.
¹² "What do you think? If a man has a hundred sheep, and one of them goes astray, does he not leave the ninety-nine and go to the mountains to seek the one that is straying?
¹³ "And if he should find it, assuredly, I say to you, he rejoices more over that *sheep* than over the ninety-nine that did not go astray.

[14] "Even so it is not the will of your Father who is in heaven that one of these little ones should perish.

## HOW TO HANDLE OFFENSES

[15] "Moreover if your brother sins against you, go and tell him his fault between you and him alone. If he hears you, you have gained your brother.
[16] "But if he will not hear, take with you one or two more, that *'by the mouth of two or three witnesses every word may be established.'*
[17] "And if he refuses to hear them, tell *it* to the church. But if he refuses even to hear the church, let him be to you like a heathen and a tax collector.

## THE POWER OF HARMONY AND AGREEMENT

[18] "Assuredly, I say to you, whatever you bind on earth will be bound in heaven, and whatever you loose on earth will be loosed in heaven.
[19] "Again I say to you that if two of you agree on earth concerning anything that they ask, it will be done for them by My Father in heaven.
[20] "For where two or three are gathered together in My name, I am there in the midst of them."

## HOW MANY TIMES ARE WE TO FORGIVE?

[21] Then Peter came to Him and said, "Lord, how often shall my brother sin against me, and I forgive him? Up to seven times?"
[22] Jesus said to him, "I do not say to you, up to seven times, but up to seventy times seven.

## THE ABSOLUTE NEED TO FORGIVE

[23] "Therefore the kingdom of heaven is like a certain king who wanted to settle accounts with his servants.
[24] "And when he had begun to settle accounts, one was brought to him who owed him ten thousand talents.
[25] "But as he was not able to pay, his master commanded that he be sold, with his wife and children and all that he had, and that payment be made.

26 "The servant therefore fell down before him, saying, 'Master, have patience with me, and I will pay you all.'

27 "Then the master of that servant was moved with compassion, released him, and forgave him the debt.

28 "But that servant went out and found one of his fellow servants who owed him a hundred denarii; and he laid hands on him and took *him* by the throat, saying, 'Pay me what you owe!'

29 "So his fellow servant fell down at his feet and begged him, saying, 'Have patience with me, and I will pay you all.'

30 "And he would not, but went and threw him into prison till he should pay the debt.

31 "So when his fellow servants saw what had been done, they were very grieved, and came and told their master all that had been done.

32 "Then his master, after he had called him, said to him, 'You wicked servant! I forgave you all that debt because you begged me.

33 'Should you not also have had compassion on your fellow servant, just as I had pity on you?'

34 "And his master was angry, and delivered him to the torturers until he should pay all that was due to him.

35 "So My heavenly Father also will do to you if each of you, from his heart, does not forgive his brother his trespasses."

# THE UNAVOIDABLE PROBLEM
## OF OFFENSES

Jesus said,

"Woe to the world because of offenses! For offenses <u>MUST</u> come."
*(Matthew 18.7 NKJV)*

and

"It is IMPOSSIBLE that no offenses will come." *(Luke 17.1 NKJV)*

The word "**impossible**" can also be translated with words and phrases like "necessary", "inevitable", or, "there must be". In other words, Jesus is telling us that it is impossible for any of us not to be offended at times in our lives. And further, times will come when even we ourselves will offend others.

The word "**offenses**" can be translated with words and phrases such as "temptations", "snares", "causes of stumbling", "pitfalls", and "influences to do wrong".

It is not IF we will be offended, but WHERE, WHEN, and HOW we will be offended. And the greater question arising out of this reality is, HOW WILL YOU AND I HANDLE OUR OFFENSES and the inevitable hurt and destruction that can come with them?

To stop the hurts of offenses from stopping us it is essential to understand what offenses are, where they come from, and what will really work in overcoming their destructive effects in our life.

## THE TWO BASIC KINDS OF OFFENSES

**DELIBERATE OFFENSES** *(Planned or Intentional)*. The word "offense" as Jesus used it in these Scriptures is a strong word in the Greek implying a deliberately laid trap. Jesus is telling us that because of the sinful nature of man there will be deliberate, premeditated traps to make people stumble and to hurt others and they are impossible to avoid or stop. They will come. All of us will experience them *(for a few examples of this type of offense see Psalms 35.11-21, 69.1-21, and 109.1-5).*

**UNPLANNED OFFENSES** *(Unintentional).* If deliberate and intentional offenses are impossible to avoid how much more is this true of the unintentional? A person says one thing and the other person interprets it as something very different and is offended. A gesture intended as a courtesy is seen as malice and offense occurs. An absence of words or deeds due to distraction or a lack of knowledge is interpreted as deliberate avoidance and offense is born. And so it is in so many ways.

During the earthly ministry of Jesus many offenses occurred on numerous occasions from His teachings, works, and living. Not deliberately (except when He was purposely confronting wrong thinking). Unintentionally. Not so much by Him, but much more so in those with a biased heart that heard and saw Him.

The offenses coming from misunderstanding Him (or, for understanding Him at other times) were numerous and deep enough that Jesus stated

"And blessed is he who is not offended because of Me." *(Matthew 11.6 NKJV)*

The truth is it does not matter where you go, or how many churches or situations you run back and forth to in seeking the ideal one, or thinking that a new spouse would be better, or that you need a better friend. It will be the same everywhere. Sooner or later there will be those unavoidable occasions of stumbling and offense causing hurt and disappointment.

The day comes when you have to have a personal face-to-face confrontation with this reality. And when that day comes you will either stop and defeat the offenses with their deadly fall-out and crushing hurts, or they will stop and defeat you.

## THE PARTIAL-KNOWLEDGE PROBLEM

One of the primary reasons intentional and unintentional offenses occur is because

"we know in PART, and we prophesy in PART" *(I Cor. 13.9 NKJV)*

and

"NOW we see through a glass DARKLY" *(I Corinthians 13.12 KJV)*

"For now we are looking in a mirror that gives only a dim (blurred) reflection [of reality as in a riddle or enigma]..." *(I Corinthians 13.12 Amplified Bible)*

Thank God, the day is coming when we will have full and complete knowledge.

"But WHEN that which is PERFECT *[complete, full]** has come, THEN that which is in PART *[imperfect, incomplete]** will be done away" *(I Corinthians 13.10 NKJV)*
*Note: the above [ ] brackets and words are inserted by the author.*

However, until "WHEN" and "THEN" comes we live HERE and "NOW" knowing only in "PART" and seeing, as it were, "DARKLY" or "only a DIM (blurred) reflection". Therefore offenses occur.

Offenses would not occur if our knowledge was complete and we could see everything clearly. But at the present time our knowledge is partial and clouded. There are dark or dim areas in our knowing.

And in these dark and dim areas of knowledge our imaginations and suspicions fill in the blanks. And thus offenses arise and over time, if not Scripturally dealt with, become strongholds of ill-will in our soul and imaginations.

Again, go back to the statement that Jesus made when He said,

... "It is inevitable that stumbling blocks come, but woe to him through whom they come!" *(Luke 17.1 NASB95)*

A noted Bible scholar paraphrased that Scriptures like this: *"In the nature of things there must be pitfalls"*. It is the nature of things as they are now that brings about these offenses, these hurts, these deep grievances.

Since the nature of things as it is now results in inevitable offenses and since our knowledge is in part, blurred, and incomplete we must choose to look to God and draw from His knowledge and wisdom that is complete and more than sufficient for the need.

Just as Adam and Eve faced the choice of what their primary source of knowledge would be *(Genesis 2.8-9, 15-17; 3.1-19)*, God or something or someone else, we also face a similar choice. Will our primary source of knowledge come from God's Word or a tree with a lying serpent in it? One source brings light and life. The other brings darkness and death.

## Both Habitual and Intentional Offenses Are Unacceptable to God

Jesus solemnly instructs all His followers that we must do everything possible to reduce the occasions of stumbling and offenses coming from our lives. The consequences of being a habitual and intentional offender is so serious that Jesus tells us that no cost is too great to pay in removing these offenses and their causes from our lives.

[6] "But whoever causes one of these little ones who believe in Me to sin, it would be better for him if a millstone were hung around his neck, and he were drowned in the depth of the sea.

[7] "Woe to the world because of offenses! For offenses must come, but woe to that man by whom the offense comes!

[8] "If your hand or foot causes you to sin, cut it off and cast *it* from you. It is better for you to enter into life lame or maimed, rather than having two hands or two feet, to be cast into the everlasting fire.

[9] "And if your eye causes you to sin, pluck it out and cast *it* from you. It is better for you to enter into life with one eye, rather than having two eyes, to be cast into hell fire" *(Matthew 18.6-9 NKJV)*.

Still, offenses do come. Every one of us experience them. In our homes. In our marriages. On our jobs. In our church life. Among our friends. In our neighborhoods and communities. Certainly from those who become our enemy. And within ourselves. There is no escape from the inevitable offenses of life. They are IMPOSSIBLE to avoid "NOW" in the present nature of things.

As careful as we might be we stumble over something or someone from time to time. And in addition we will cause someone to stumble. Mostly un-intentionally rather than intentionally, but still sometime, some place, we will offend and cause someone to stumble.

Every child of God earnestly seeking to walk in God's light strives and works to become mature in the things of God. Offenses do diminish in number as maturity in Christ progresses in our lives, but offenses are still with us in all areas of living. So what can we do about them?

God calls us to develop a frame of mind and a temperament of heart that will minimize offenses; a mind-set and heart disposition that will turn stumbling stones into stepping stones. But how do we accomplish this?

## DEALING WITH OFFENSES

Our Lord Jesus Christ came to help and save both the offended and the offender.

"For the Son of Man has come to save that which was lost"
*(See Matthew 18.11–14 NKJV).*

There is help and deliverance for all. That one lost sheep straying from the fold is the intense object of His salvation search. It is not our Father's will that any should perish:

"The Lord is not slack concerning *His* promise, as some count slackness, but is longsuffering toward us, not willing that any should perish but that all should come to repentance" *(II Peter 3.9 NKJV).*

It is God's unmistakable will that none perish and all come to repentance. Thank God our sinful offenses toward Him and toward His are forgiven through the blood of His Son, Jesus Christ, when we respond to the Holy Spirit's work within us and we repent in faith and ask forgiveness.

When we are saved God's spiritual DNA, so to speak, and power is imparted to us that is more than sufficient to enable everyone to overcome being a habitual and intentional offender. That same DNA power enables us to overcome being destroyed by offenses as well.

"I can do all things through Christ who strengthens me." *(Philippians 4.13 NKJV)*

Paul experienced this wonderful salvation power and in his own words said,

"And I thank Christ Jesus our Lord, who has ENABLED me, because he counted me faithful, putting me into the ministry; although I was formerly a blasphemer, and a PERSECUTOR, and an insolent* man: but I obtained mercy, because I did it ignorantly in unbelief. And the grace of our Lord was exceedingly abundant, with faith and love which are in Christ Jesus" *(I Timothy 1.12–14 NKJV)* *violently arrogant – variant reading.

In this passage of Scripture Paul plainly states that before his salvation he was intentionally trying to stop anyone that was a follower of Christ. In fact, he thought he was helping God by doing so when he was actually, in

11

ignorance and unintentionally, injuring God's people and work. Then Jesus saved him! He was delivered from being an offender. His offenses were forgiven.

God's Salvation that brings forgiveness is the distinct way God Himself begins in dealing with our problems of offenses and stumbling. A beginning. There remains much that must flow out of our salvation if our plight of offenses is to become a victorious one in Scriptural completeness.

Jesus clearly taught us to pray

"And forgive us our debts, As we forgive our debtors" *(Matthew 6.12 NKJV)*

Another translation of that verse reads:

"And forgive us our debts, as we also have forgiven (left, remitted, and let go of the debts, and have given up resentment against) our debtors." *(Matthew 6.12 Amplified Bible)*

God deals with our sins and offenses against Him and heaven by the means of forgiveness—and it has been working for thousands of years in countless millions of lives.

Because of God's divine approach of forgiveness in dealing with our sinful offenses John the Apostle declared,

"I looked, and behold, a great multitude which no one could number of all nations, tribes, peoples, and tongues...clothed with white robes" who had "washed their robes and made them white in the blood of the Lamb" *(see Revelation 7.9–17 NKJV).*

If this divine approach of forgiveness is powerful enough to get us into heaven for all eternity surely it is able to get us through a few years of temporal offenses in life here on earth.

## THREE BASIC STEPS IN DEALING WITH OFFENSES

In Matthew 18.15-17 Jesus gives us three steps in dealing with and bringing resolve to offenses. I will identify them as: **The Private Step**, **The Semi-Private Step**, and **The Public Step**.

## 1. THE PRIVATE STEP

"Moreover if your brother sins against you, go and tell him his fault between you and him alone. If he hears you, you have gained your brother" *(Matthew 18.15 NKJV)*.

Jesus clearly instructs us to go to the offender, the one who has trespassed against us creating a debt owed to us (a debt in the sense of owing us an apology, amends, compensation, etc) and to PRIVATELY seek to work it out.

Little if any good is served by making offenses public and displaying them before everyone. Jesus knows the human personality *(see John 2.24–25)*. When we publicly expose and humiliate others we only solidify them in their offensive behavior making true resolve more difficult than ever.

But I know by years of experience that the Word of God works. I deeply believe that the majority of all offenses can be worked out privately when we seriously listen to and follow the Lord's instructions on dealing with offenses that maim and destroy lives.

I have also observed over the years that one reason the private step is bypassed or treated with insignificance is due to a person wanting things to be made public for purposes of revenge, vengeance, and humiliation (although these words would rarely if ever be used by the person not wanting an offense settled privately). Yet another reason is the selfish desire to make one's self look good at the expense of another.

## 2. THE SEMI-PRIVATE STEP

"But if he will not hear you, take with you one or two more, that *'by the mouth of two or three witnesses every word may be established.'"* *(Matthew 18.16 NKJV)*

Only when the problem of offense and trespass cannot be worked out privately does it become necessary to involve *"one or two more"* persons in seeking to bring proper resolve to the situation.

Obviously these should be persons that both you and the offender along with others respect and have confidence in. They certainly should not be gossipmongers or the like.

It is clear from the overall Scriptures in God's Word that you would want to take with you people of prayer who are filled with the Holy Spirit and wisdom. You are seeking resolve, not exposure and further offense.

This step could have been called the Semi-PUBLIC Step since it goes outside of the offender and the offended. However, I believe, privacy is still the tone here although there is Scriptural preparation made in the event that it should have to become a public matter for the church.

This is all the more reason the witnesses should be those of absolute trust and integrity.

Hopefully, if the matter goes this far, it can be prayerfully resolved at this point AFTER you have earnestly and sincerely pursued the private step that Jesus instructs us to use first.

## 3. THE PUBLIC STEP

"And if he refuses to hear them, tell *it* to the church. But if he refuses even to hear the church, let him be to you like a heathen and a tax collector" *(Matthew 18.17 NKJV).*

There are occasions (that, thank God, are ever so rare) when after the PRIVATE and SEMI-PRIVATE steps do not bring proper resolve it may become necessary that the offense must become or will become public and known by many. This is when the Scriptural discipline of verse 17 has to be applied so that the offense does not spread like a poison and destroy other innocent lives and experiences with the Lord.

But even then, it is still a matter of Scriptural discipline which is designed to bring about restoration and correction, not an item for carnal gossip that never restores or corrects.

Concerning the words of Jesus that say, *"let him be to you like a heathen and a tax collector"*, remember that Matthew, the writer of this passage of Scripture and the entire Gospel that it is found in, was a publican (that is, a tax collector), and Jesus Himself in His ministry of love and forgiveness made Matthew an apostle *(also, see Matthew 21.32, Mark 2.15-16, Luke 5.29-30, 15.1).*

There is also another tax collector named Zacchaeus *(Luke 19.1-10)* that Jesus redeemed from offenses and being an offender. The outcome is thus recorded:

"Then Zacchaeus stood and said to the Lord, 'Look, Lord, I give half of my goods to the poor; and if I have taken anything from anyone by false accusation, I **restore** fourfold.' And Jesus said to him, 'Today salvation has come to this house...for the Son of Man has come to seek and save that which was lost'" *(Luke 19.8–10 NKJV).*

It is at this point and in the following Scriptures of Matthew 18 that Jesus brings us to forgiveness as the ultimate way of dealing with offenses. But first there is one more truth we need to consider and understand.

# BINDING AND LOOSENING
## (RETAINING AND RELEASING)

[18] "Assuredly, I say to you, whatever you bind on earth will be bound in heaven, and whatever you loose on earth will be loosed in heaven.
[19] "Again I say to you that if two of you agree on earth concerning anything that they ask, it will be done for them by My Father in heaven.
[20] "For where two or three are gathered together in My name, I am there in the midst of them" (Matthew 18.18–20 NKJV).

Here we come to a powerful and timely truth that I feel the Lord was showing me that Saturday morning mentioned earlier in my introduction, *The Beginning of the Journey*.

All through my ministry, from the time I was nineteen years old, I have predominantly heard verses 18 through 20 of Matthew, chapter 18, used in connection with healing, casting out demons, and a deliverance type application. Once or so I read of it in connection with church discipline (which is the immediate context here).

Now I was seeing in these very Scriptures how we can bind and loose our lives by our attitudes of forgiveness and unforgiveness toward offenses. As I briefly stated in my introduction I personally experienced this binding and loosening when I began to apply the principles and dynamics of forgiveness *(also see testimonies one and five at the close of Section 6 for more on Binding and Loosing)*.

I am not saying that there isn't a divine principle and directive here that can be applicable to other areas such as healing, deliverance, and the like because I believe there is. I also believe this is true of and applicable to other demonic obstacles, sinful situations, and hindrances to the work of God as well.

But now I was seeing that the immediate and primary reference of these Scriptures was speaking of another powerful and forceful truth having to do with offenses given and/or taken and the responses from us that God looks for.

By forgiving we can literally bind the forces and influences of our fallen flesh-nature and the satanic/demonic power of darkness while at the same time, in a sense, loosening the power of the Holy Spirit to more fully flow in our life and in the lives of others.

Unforgiveness binds the flow of God's fuller blessings inherent in the Word of God, the fuller working of the Holy Spirit coming to us from the Father through salvation in His Son Jesus, and our faith, so that the needed resolve cannot come to lives in the fullness that is needed, and loosens the sinful flesh-nature and demonic powers to destroy in a greater measure!

This is what was happening in my life when God began to awaken my heart to the dynamics of forgiveness and unforgiveness. It happened as I began releasing through forgiveness those who had offended me that those areas of my life bound by the hurts of offenses and unforgiveness were loosed. Then a much fuller work of the Holy Spirit began flowing in both my personal life and ministry.

Our speaking and agreeing together—that is, aligning our thinking and believing—with what God says in His Word on forgiveness loosens and liberates our soul and the souls of others from the binding hurts of offenses.

Our speaking and agreeing together with what others say or think in unforgiveness binds and imprisons our soul and other souls in their offenses.

God's heavenly provisions of power work in their greater fullness as we loose the situation with forgiveness by taking our hands off of people and situations by placing them in God's hands.

Heaven is bound in certain, critical instances and senses, when we continue through unforgiveness to hold in our hands and hearts the offenses and the offenders!

There is some sense of this, I believe, seen in the Scripture containing the following statement of Jesus:

"So Jesus said to them again, 'Peace to you! AS the Father has sent Me, I ALSO send you.' And when He had said this, He breathed on *them,* and said to them, 'Receive the HOLY Spirit. If you FORGIVE the sins of any, they are forgiven them; if you RETAIN the *sins* of any, they are retained'" *(John 20.21–23 NKJV).*

The Holy Spirit longs to work fully in our local churches, but there are so many areas that are bound by unforgiveness toward hurts and offenses! God deeply desires to bless our homes and marriages in far greater measure, but He is deterred because of bitterness we are harboring toward our spouses, children, parents, other family members, or, anyone or anything due to unforgiveness.

As results, destruction abounds where there should and could be construction. Division where there could be unity. Sickness of the heart and mind where there could be healing. Pain where there could be peace. Despair where there could be hope. Darkness where there could be light. Sadness where there could be joy.

When these truths began coming alive and filling my heart, I saw this and other dynamics of forgiveness in a light that I had never seen before. I determined then I would not consult any of the considerable number of books (over 2,000) I had at that time in my personal library (outside of concordances and similar research books) until I was satisfied that the Lord was finished with this sudden and unexpected happening and conveying of truth going on in my life.

For days I poured over just the Scriptures. God's written Truth and Spirit of Truth communed with my heart. I listened. I wrote. I applied.

On a Thursday shortly following the Saturday morning that all of this began stirring in my life I attended a large interdenominational Christian business men's dinner and gathering in Thousand Oaks, California. A well-known minister for that time period was the featured speaker for the evening.

During the course of the speaker's message he mentioned a book written by Catherine Marshall (Peter Marshall's wife) entitled *"Something More"* that had a chapter in it on the *"Law of Generations"*. He recommended that everyone purchase the book if for nothing else than that one chapter. I had so many books that the idea of buying another one did not really appeal to me.

However, it was at this point as I sat at the head table with the chapter president, who was one of the men in my pastorate, that I sensed a quiet but definite inner nudging and impression saying: "Get that book. There is something more in there for you."

As soon as the meeting was concluded I walked over to a group of tables where a vendor was selling various books. A rather large crowd had already gathered. I asked if they had the book the speaker had mentioned. They did. However, just one was left and someone else was looking at it. I waited, feeling that I was supposed to have that book.

Then the person laid that one last and only copy down. I picked it up and thumbed through it. My heart almost leaped out of my chest. There it was. This was what I felt that the nudging in my heart was about. Chapter 3 "Forgiveness: The Aughts and Anys". I was excited and as soon as possible I started home to read it.

When at last I was home I began to eagerly read. As I read my heart began to overflow. Here were some of the very verses of Scripture that had been speaking into my heart about forgiveness.

I want to quote a relevant portion of that chapter here of a conversation between the author, Catherine Marshall, and her friend, David duPlessis:

...in 1971, at a time when certain family prayers were still unanswered, David gave us an insight as powerful as the "[God has] no grandsons" one.

Over coffee in our living room he pointed out to us a verse of scripture that had long puzzled me:

"Verily I say unto you, whatsoever ye shall bind on earth shall be bound in heaven: and whatsoever ye shall loose on earth shall be loosed in heaven."

"For a long time I was puzzled," David told us, "about what 'loosing' and 'binding' meant. Then I found out: it means that by hanging onto my judgment of another, I can bind him to the very conditions I'd like to see changed.

"By our unforgiveness, we stand between the other person and the Holy Spirit's work in convicting him and then helping him. By stepping out of the way through releasing somebody from our judgment, we're not necessarily saying, 'He's right and I'm wrong.' Forgiveness means, 'He can be as wrong as wrong can be, but I'll not be the judge.' Forgiveness means that I'm no longer binding a certain person on earth. It means withholding judgment.

"How I wish," David continued, "that I'd been taught that from the beginning. My whole Christian life would have been different. Judge, judge—there are no more judgmental people in the world than Christians. It was certainly so in my life! When the Lord made me face up to that, He told me, 'You're not forgiving... You're a public prosecutor, judging everybody in sight. And I want you to be a public defender—not a public prosecutor.'"

David put down his cup of coffee. "Weren't you and Len telling me that you're troubled by some unanswered prayers? Well, in my life I've found this forgiveness business a key to getting prayers answered. A couple of years ago I was going through one of those prayers-not-getting-beyond-the-ceiling periods and I prayed, 'Lord, I don't have enough faith. Give me the gift of faith.'

"'It isn't your faith,' the reply came. 'I can see faith even if it's as small as a mustard seed. No, it's something else...When you stand praying—forgive if ye have aught against any. That's your trouble. That's why your prayers aren't answered. You go about with a lot of aughts against a lot of anys.'"

As David concluded his story, I thought to myself, "Our aughts against all the anys...What a shaft of light!" So now we saw why certain of our prayers had not been answered and we set ourselves to the work of forgiveness.*

---

* From *Something More* by Catherine Marshall LeSourd, pp. 37–39, Copyright © 1974 by Catherine Marshall LeSourd. Used with permission of McGraw-Hill Book Company.

In the mouth of two or three witnesses! I could hardly sit still as I read. I called my wife over. I read this quote to her and then excitedly related to her the things about forgiveness that I felt the Lord had been revealing to my heart.

Now I knew for certain that I was on an appointed path to a fresh insight and understanding in an area vital to the heart of our Father and the well-being of our self, marriage, home, family, church, and the like. FORGIVENESS IS GOD'S ULTIMATE IN DEALING WITH OFFENSES AND DEEP GRIEVANCES!

The personal and Private Step can work wonders. The Semi- Private Step can bring resolve. The Public Step of Scriptural discipline can bring about correction. But when all is said and done, forgiveness must be our ultimate and final way of dealing with offenses against our lives whether as a collective group or as an individual.

We bind people to their undesirable conditions by being judgmental and unforgiving! The more we speak and agree with others on it, the more binding the situation becomes.

And, thank God, we can loose the situations of offenses by forgiving.

"And whenever you stand praying, FORGIVE, if you have AUGHT against ANY" *(Mark 11.25 KJV).*

Nothing brings the ultimate victory that nullifies offenses, the demonic, and the sinful flesh-nature like forgiveness. Forgiveness binds Satan's evil intents and loosens the fullness of God's provisions in heaven and on earth to work in our lives.

There was a situation in the Corinthian church that is referred to by Paul in II Corinthians that helps illustrate what I am speaking of here. The situation involved an offending brother in the Corinthian church that they had to take the public step number three in Dealing with Offenses.

It had resulted in a disciplinary action concerning a man who is unknown to us, but obviously was well known to the Corinthian church. Paul says:

[6] "This punishment which was inflicted by the majority is sufficient for such a man,

[7] so that, on the contrary, you ought rather to FORGIVE and comfort him, lest perhaps such a one be swallowed up with too much sorrow.

[8] Therefore I urge you to reaffirm your love to him.

[9] For to this end I also wrote, that I might put you to the test, whether you are obedient in all things.

¹⁰ Now whom you FORGIVE anything, I also FORGIVE. For if indeed I have FORGIVEN anything, I have FORGIVEN that one for your sakes in the presence of Christ,
**¹¹ lest Satan should take advantage of us; for we are not ignorant of his devices** *(II Corinthians 2.6–11 NKJV).*

## — THE ULTIMATE OF FORGIVENESS —
## IS FORGIVENESS REALLY ALL THAT IMPORTANT?

As you look at the entire eighteenth chapter of Matthew you will see that the disciples earnestly sought to understand what Jesus was saying. Every verse in the chapter ties in with the seriousness of offenses, the steps in dealing with offenses, and forgiveness.

Listen to what Peter asked after listening to Jesus talk about the impossibility and seriousness of offenses, about the private, semi-private and public steps in dealing with them, and about binding and loosing:

"THEN came Peter to him, and said, Lord, how often shall my brother SIN AGAINST me, and I FORGIVE him? till seven times?" *(Matthew 18.21 NKJV)*

Jesus understood exactly what Peter was asking in the light of what had just been taught.

"Jesus said to him, 'I do not say to you, up to seven times, but up to seventy times seven!'" *(Matthew 18.22 NKJV)*

Note here that Jesus' response does not put any condition upon our forgiveness. Later in the book we will look at why we can <u>NOT</u> have conditions on our forgiveness—although God can and does place conditions on His forgiveness in our lives. Our forgiveness is to be unconditional. Until seventy times seven! This is another way of saying, "Every time!"

But again, is forgiveness really all that important? Consider the parable Jesus used as an illustration and it will answer this question.

## JESUS' PARABLE OF THE OFFENDING
## UNFORGIVING FORGIVEN SERVANT
## (MATTHEW 18.23-35)

To reinforce what Jesus was saying about forgiveness being the ultimate in dealing with offenses and its vital necessity, Jesus gave us one of the most thought-provoking and disturbing of all His earthly parables. Some try to weaken and water it down, but it only stands out stronger and more pointed when so treated. Jesus left no room for questions. He said what He meant and He meant what He said.

<sup>23</sup> "THEREFORE the kingdom of heaven is like a certain king who wanted to settle accounts with his servants.

<sup>24</sup> "And when he had begun to settle accounts, one was brought to him who owed him 10,000 talents *[about $10,000,000 – Amplified Bible]*.

<sup>25</sup> "But as HE WAS NOT ABLE TO PAY, his master commanded that he be sold, with his wife and children and all that he had, and that payment be made.

<sup>26</sup> "The servant therefore fell down before him, saying, 'Master, have patience with me, and I will pay you all.'

<sup>27</sup> "Then the master of that servant was moved with compassion, RELEASED him, and FORGAVE him the debt." *(Matthew 18.23-27 NKJV).*

In this parable Jesus uses a story about an offending servant who owed his king a debt of what would be comparable today to approximately ten million dollars.

The king demanded that the man repay, but he could not. What was to be done about this tremendous outrage, offense, and debt to the throne? Simple. By the laws and customs of that day, sell the servant, his wife, his children, everything he has, and apply it against the debt of offense.

Please note that this man's home, family, and marriage were also involved in the consequences and fall-out of his offense.

The servant pleaded and begged to save his home and loved ones — and himself! The king was *"moved with compassion, and RELEASED [i.e., LOOSED or FREED – author's note] him, and FORGAVE him the debt."*

Forgiveness was the king's ultimate way in dealing with the servant's offense. In fact, it was the only way if that man and his family were ever to be free and not be bound to prison and slavery. How many of us could begin, even today, to repay a debt like this?

Forgiveness saved this man. Forgiveness saved his family. What joy must have filled the servant's heart and those of his family. How wonderful the liberty of forgiveness is! He was completely free. Nothing now stood between him and his king, their fellowship, and work together. He was now a FORGIVEN SERVANT!

However, the story does not end here.

The day after our miracle always comes! Like it did for the man lame from birth in Acts 3 that earned his income by begging at the Gate Beautiful. *After* he was miraculously *loosed* from his lifetime of paralysis, and *after* the shouting, leaping, and rejoicing *the day after his miracle came.* And more days followed after that. He no longer had a disability of paralysis to justify his raising an income by begging. Traveling, giving his testimony, and taking an offering would last only a season. His attitude, thinking, life-style, and way of day-to-day living would have to change. More was now expected of him by both God and people because *he was enabled by God to live differently.*

> ## The day after our miracle always comes!

So it is for all of us. And so it was for this forgiven servant in Jesus' parable. Look what happened in the days after his miracle.

28 "But that servant went out and found one of his fellow servants who owed him a hundred denarii *[about $25 – Amplified Bible]*; and he laid hands on him and took *him* by the throat, saying, 'Pay me what you owe!'
29 "So his fellow servant fell down at his feet and begged him, saying, 'Have patience with me, and I will pay you all.'
30 "And he would not, but went and threw him into prison till he should pay the debt." *(Matthew 18.28-30 NKJV)*

Jesus tells us that the day(s) after he was released by forgiveness from his own un-payable debt that the forgiven servant went out and found one of his fellow servants that owed him a debt of offense. It really wasn't much in comparison with the ten-million-dollar-debt he himself had owed to the king and had been freely forgiven of. In fact, it was only about twenty-five dollars in all owed by this fellow Offending-Servant to the Forgiven-Servant.

Isn't this like the way our offenses toward one another are compared to our forgiven offenses toward our Great King and Heavenly Father!

Jesus said the Ten-Million-Dollar-Forgiven-Servant then took his Fellow-Twenty-Five-Dollar-Offending-Servant by the throat demanding payment be made at once or else. Unforgiveness always turns ugly—even violent and vicious!

The Fellow-Twenty-Five-Dollar-Offending-Servant begged for time just as the Ten-Million-Dollar-Forgiven-Servant had done. The Ten-Million-Dollar-Forgiven-Servant would not listen. What will he do about this twenty-five dollar offense?

Cast the Fellow-Twenty-Five-Dollar-Offending-Servant into jail! That is, BIND him! Bind him to a condition that he will likely never be able to correct in jail. Bind him to the debt for a life time. Give no quarter. Justice must be done and served. This Fellow-Twenty-Five-Dollar-Offending-Servant is worthy of retribution and vengeance! Surely everyone could see this.

So the Fellow-Twenty-Five-Dollar-Offending-Servant was BOUND with and in unforgiveness by the Ten-Million-Dollar-Forgiven-Servant.

The conclusion of this parable is a truth that we all should learn and never forget. Look and listen carefully to Jesus here.

[31] "So when his fellow servants saw what had been done, they were very grieved, and came and told their master all that had been done.

[32] "Then his master, after he had called him, said to him, 'You wicked servant! I forgave you all that debt because you begged me.

[33] 'Should you not also have had compassion on your fellow servant, just as I had pity on you?'

[34] "And his master was angry, and delivered him to the torturers until he should pay all that was due to him" (Matthew 18.31-35 NKJV).

When the king heard what the Ten-Million-Dollar-Unforgiving-Forgiven-Servant had done to his offending fellow servant he was extremely angry. The king then had the Ten-Million-Dollar-Unforgiving-Forgiven-Servant taken and delivered to the "torturers" (tormentors) until he should repay all of his debt to the throne. There is no peace where there is unforgiveness. There is only torturous torment.

The double tragedy was this: not only was the Twenty-Five-Dollar-Offending-Servant bound and his home and friends affected, but so was the Ten-Million-Dollar-Unforgiving-Forgiven-Servant along with the loss to his own wife, children, home, and friends!

Unforgiveness always binds. It binds everyone, everywhere, every time, in every way! Always unforgiveness makes it impossible for the King of Glory to work fully in our lives.

Hear carefully Jesus' own words of application in His conclusion of the parable.

"So My heavenly Father also will do to you if each of you, from his heart, does not forgive his brother his trespasses." *(Matthew 18.35 NKJV)*

It has been well said by many over the years: "The one thing God cannot and will not forgive is an unforgiving heart."

God help us not to be like many who heard Jesus' parables but never understood them. God help us to have ears to hear and hearts that are softly pliable to His tender touch.

This powerful truth became a burning realization in my heart! There will be no full continuing and lasting renewal of the Holy Spirit in our churches, homes, marriages, and hearts until there is a genuine release of forgiveness flowing in the interpersonal relationships of our everyday life that brings God's indispensible healing for the many inevitable offenses that will invade our lives.

There may be spurts and dribbles of blessings, but there will be no flowing rivers. Unforgiveness chokes-off the flowing rivers of God's blessings and work in myriads of lives, homes, and churches in our nation. Unforgiveness binds and squeezes the full flowing provisions of God's power down to a trickle of what it could and should be.

## GOD'S SPACE OF GRACE

"...are you [so blind as to] trifle with and presume upon and despise and underestimate the wealth of His kindness and forbearance and long-suffering patience? Are you unmindful or actually ignorant [of the fact] that God's kindness is intended to lead you to repent (to change your mind and inner man to accept God's will)?" *(Romans 2.4 Amplified Bible)*

This Scripture in Romans speaks of not fully grasping what those occasional trickling down of God's blessings and goodness are sent to accomplish in the heart bound in unforgiveness.

When God blesses us in His kindness and forbearance He is not overlooking our sin or trespass of unforgiveness and the accompanying sins that go with it. He is blessing us as stated in Romans 2.4 with a **SPACE OF GRACE** to repent, to find divine deliverance, and forgiveness.

If you are confused at your present situation in which you find one day marked with blessing and the next, so to speak, empty, it just may be that God is reaching out to you to repent of the unforgiveness and the sins it gives birth to that are binding the continuous full flow of His presence and work in your life!

24

Those spasmodic blessings in your life may very well be God speaking through His goodness, forbearance, and longsuffering to bring you to the place of repentance from what is preventing forgiveness toward offenses that lay buried like a hidden cancer in your life.

## MY FORGIVENESS AWAKENING

A few months before the Holy Spirit began that Saturday morning work spoken of in my introduction, *The Beginning of the Journey*, I had looked around my home. I saw several beautiful gifts and plaques that different ones had given to my wife and me during the pastorate of that time.

Suddenly, a feeling came over me. A bad feeling. Several of those that had given us gifts had later caused us great anguish and pain. I felt they had betrayed our trust and confidence in them. They had sought, I felt, to destroy us—especially me. The feeling began to grow (or more correctly, come to the surface).

I looked over at my wife and in anger said, "I feel like taking every one of those presents, wrapping them up, and sending them back to those who gave them to us. They betrayed us. They turned on our friendship."

My wife was shocked. "Honey", she said, "I have never heard you say things like that about people before. I have never seen you feeling this way." It wasn't just the words she had spoken. It was the emotion she had said it with. And the way it had come out of me that had affected her. I had spoken and given voice to the unforgiveness I had hidden in my heart!

Suddenly I realized what was there. In my heart. Bitterness. Unforgiveness. Blinding and binding. Hidden like a cancer starting to spread, to kill, and destroy.

Oh, with some effort I thought I had managed to get over it. But all I really had done was just bury it. The trouble with turning weeds under rather than uprooting them is that they will grow again. The roots that remain will bear life again. They are just hidden, not gone. Dormant for a time, not dead.

When the proper times and conditions come they will come to life and sprout again breaking through the surface to mar, choke, and bind the beautiful and beneficial plantings of

> The trouble with turning weeds under rather than uprooting them is that they will grow again.

God's Word and Spirit. Like the thorny places in Jesus' parable of the sower, the seed, and the soil *(Matthew 13.22, Mark 4.18–19, and Luke 8.14).*

Now the time had come on that Saturday chosen by God I spoke of previously. As the truth began to stir my heart about these aspects of the dynamics of forgiveness, I was made aware that it was for the shepherd as well as the flock. All of these unforgiving feelings and attitudes began to surface.

Then the Holy Spirit began opening my life up just like a anatomical dissection. From the crown of my head to the soles of my feet. All the way. He cut and laid me open exposing all the parts and pieces.

For the word of God is living and powerful, and sharper than any two-edged sword, piercing even to the division of soul and spirit, and of joints and marrow, and is a discerner of the thoughts and intents of the heart. *(Hebrews 4.12 NKJV)*

I began to see not just these recent events, but numerous events of many years standing that had gone out of sight but had never really been forgiven. I mean really Scripturally forgiven.

## WHERE MUST THIS FORGIVENESS START?

I began to realize that forgiveness in a home, the life of a church, or in the numerous life relationships we have must start somewhere, at some time, with someone in order for Hell to be bound and Heaven to be loosed on earth. But where, when, and with whom does it start?

Yes, I know forgiveness started with God. But the problem we have at present is forgiveness does not often get too far past that point in our lives.

The question is where does forgiveness start—here and now? At this place and point in our lives. Since we ourselves have been forgiven and saved.

Probably many of you are thinking just as I did, "I am a good and considerate person. I am a Christian. Just as soon as the ones who have offended me come to me, humble themselves, wash my feet with their tears, dry them with their hair, confess their meanness and wrong doing, then I will graciously and lovingly forgive them."

High and mighty us! God help us. As I briefly indicated previously, only God has a right to set and demand conditions on forgiveness. We have no right to do so.

Have you ever noticed that there are precious few incidents recorded where people came to Jesus and asked for forgiveness, but He freely spoke forgiveness and forgave throughout His life and ministry as He saw what was truly happening in people's hearts. They sought forgiveness through their actions rather than just words.

God's truth spoke to my heart. The ministry of forgiveness in our particular congregation was to begin with me. With my first message to my flock I confessed and asked forgiveness. In my private prayers, since God had exposed the bitterness and unforgiveness hidden inside of me, I had already been calling out the names and incidents of offenses that had occurred from the present all the way back into the years of my past.

Release came! A glorious loosening. It really worked. I began to receive cards with notations from people that would, I believe, never have written to me asking my forgiveness. I was overwhelmed and humbled. They did not realize that weeks before I had already had to ask the Lord to forgive me for my feelings of ill will and unforgiveness against them. I responded with joy in my heart to their cards and notations. Forgiveness began when I began with the Lord painfully but honestly. What peace and happiness followed and has continued since.

God forgave and canceled my ten million dollars in debt of offense completely and freely because of Christ. Because of Christ I completely and freely canceled every twenty-five dollars and every twenty-five cents in debt of offense I felt was owed to me.

I released people and I released things through forgiveness. When I released them then the Holy Spirit was "loosed" or "released" to move in and begin His fuller work in my life and ministry.

You cannot clearly see Jesus as long as you have other people and things between you and Him. It is only when you release these other people and cancel their debt through forgiveness that you can again see Jesus in His fullness because others are no longer between you and Him.

I realize that there may be those who owe you what looks like an enormous debt, but is it anything compared with the debt you and I owed to God? Again, like twenty-five dollars compared with ten million dollars?

There were people who I felt owed me a debt! The Lord was saying in effect to me, "I want you to cancel ALL the debts real or imagined of every single person and circumstance and wipe the books clear. Walk away from it and release them to Me to work in your life and theirs." When I did, He did! When you will, He will! It was like the Year of Jubilee in my life *(see Leviticus 27)*.

Here I want to make an interesting observation with you. We must be careful not to entertain a thought similar to that of James and John when the Samaritans refused Jesus and His disciples a place to spend the evening in their town. James and John were offended and said:

"Lord, do You want us to command fire to come down from heaven and consume them, just as Elijah did?" *(Luke 9.54 NKJV)*

27

When we respond to offenses as James and John did it just may be us that winds up burned by the fires of discipline from God. Jesus would say to us as He did to them,

*"You do not know what manner of spirit you are of. For the Son of man did not come to DESTROY men's lives, but to SAVE them" (Luke 9.55–56 NKJV).*

After the Day of Pentecost following Jesus' death, resurrection, ascension back to heaven, John was sent from Jerusalem along with Peter to pray for the Samaritans that had turned to Christ under Phillip's ministry to receive the infilling of the Holy Spirit *(Acts 8.14–17).*

These Samaritans, I believe, could very well have been some of the very ones John and his brother James had wanted to call fire down on before Jesus' work on the cross. Now under John's ministry along with Peter they received God's Holy Spirit fire of power and blessing falling down out of heaven and filling their lives that Acts 8 day!

Wanting to see offensive people destroyed by the fires of judgment is not the attitude, heart, or ministry of forgiveness!

The release of forgiveness is not, "Oh, Lord! I release them to you. Now you take out vengeance on them for me good and proper. You do things to them Lord that I am not allowed or supposed to do. They will get what they deserve now. Wow! This forgiveness business is great. I should have tried it before."

That kind of attitude is not God's forgiveness business. That is bitterness business and hatred coming from an unforgiving heart in the disguise of pious prayer to the Throne of God—and He will not have any part of it!

Forgiveness is not trying to sneak in the back door of heaven to get a curse of destruction via heaven poured out on others, but boldly through the forgiving, cleansing blood of Jesus entering the front doors to the Throne of Grace for a release of healing waters via forgiveness that starts with us and flows out of us to others such as our offenders!

When we release people through forgiveness we cancel the debt completely. They owe us nothing. We want no kind of payment or satisfaction of revenge. We want revival. We want renewal. We want an outpouring of the Holy Spirit. Christ flowing to, in, and through us. Working through us. Ministering through us. Loving through us. Forgiving through us.

I believe it is another part of that *"fellowship of His suffering"* that leads to a greater knowledge of Who He really is and to His resurrection power! *(Compare with Philippians 3.10)*

Forgiveness is one of God's ways where we forget

"those things which are behind" and "press toward the goal...of the high calling of God in Christ Jesus" *(Philippians 3.13–14 NKJV).*

## IN FORGIVENESS WE ACKNOWLEDGE THAT JESUS IS TRULY OUR LORD!

When we forgive we do another very important thing. We say in effect, "JESUS, YOU ARE LORD. I will do what you have commanded me to do. I will do it gladly and readily even as you gladly and readily forgave me."

When we refuse or count it as insignificant to forgive we are saying in effect, "Jesus, you are not the Lord of my life. I do not care what You said! In fact, I'm not sure You really know what You are talking about. The person who has grieved me is going to pay down to the very last penny. I may even demand interest if they are too long in paying. I am going to harbor these feelings of resentment even though I am aware they could turn to a cancerous bitterness that will destroy me..."

Someone says, "I cannot forgive". This is absolutely untrue. This violates holy revelation contained in the Scriptures. It is a lie to say, "I cannot" when the Word of God declares,

"I CAN do ALL things through Christ who strengthens me" *(Philippians 4.13 NKJV).*

When we say, "I cannot", we are speaking a lie and agreeing with Satan. And Jesus said,

"...the devil...is a liar, and the father of it" *(John 8.44 NKJV).*

What we are saying in reality is not, "I cannot", but rather, "I <u>WILL</u> NOT". To say, "I cannot", is to blame God and

"make him a liar, and his word is not in us" *(I John 1.10 NKJV)*

The whole truth of the matter is I could if I would. I can if I will—versus—I can't because I won't. I couldn't because I wouldn't. This may not be the most stylish English, but it is painfully true!

Jesus never for one moment even faintly hinted that we would not be able to forgive. Read the entire eighteenth chapter of Matthew once again carefully and I believe that you will agree that Jesus is saying we can and that we must forgive!

This not to say that it is easy and does not require coming against bitterness, hate, hurt, and the like. But it is both doable and essential that we battle it through by and in the grace of God working in and through our lives to other lives.

The Psalmist beautifully observed,

"If You, Lord, should keep account of *and* treat [us according to our] sins, O Lord, who could stand? But there is forgiveness with You [just what man needs], that You may be reverently feared *and* worshiped" *(Psalms 130.3–4* Amplified Bible).

Do we want God to deal with us on the basis of a strict accounting that calls for the meticulous payment from us of every wrong doing, or, do we want Him to deal with us on the basis of His mercy, grace, and forgiveness in Jesus Christ?

How does God want us to deal with our brothers and sisters in Christ, our leaders, our family, our spouse, children, our parents, and others? I believe the answer is obvious.

# THROUGH THE ULTIMATE OF FORGIVENESS!

# THOUGHTS

1. **WHERE SIN ABOUNDS**, there offenses and offenders will abound along with hurt, pain, and anguish. And hurt and pain lead to bitterness and hate. Then bitterness and hate lead to destruction, division, and ultimately to the disease and death of our homes, marriages, friendships, churches, happiness, joy, peace, and our fellowship with the Lord. Everything of value and worth having in life grows sick and becomes anemic or perishes where there is unforgiveness.

2. **WHERE GRACE ABOUNDS**, offenses and offenders are greatly reduced. The hurt and pain we experience will drive us to prayer and cause us to pull closer to the Lord. The Lord will then lead us into love, long-suffering, and forgiveness. This then brings us into the fullness of His great salvation, healing, restoration, unity, friendship, and fellowship with our Lord while bringing strength to our home, marriage, church, and other life relationships.

3. **WHERE SIN ABOUNDS**, we are crushed by the mountains that challenge our lives. **WHERE GRACE ABOUNDS**, we crush the mountains that challenge our lives.

**WHERE SIN ABOUNDS**, we are crushed by the mountains that challenge our lives. **WHERE GRACE ABOUNDS**, we crush the mountains that challenge our lives.

## FORGIVENESS RELEASES US TO MINISTER TO OTHERS

In a marriage one of the most devastating offenses resulting in excruciating pain is that of adultery—when one spouse is unfaithful and violates their sacred marriage covenant by having illicit sexual relations with someone outside their sacred union.

In my fifty-one plus years as a pastor I have had many broken hearted husbands and wives that have come to me in one of the deepest anguishes known to the human heart—that of adultery and unfaithfulness.

Most who have come to me have been the ones violated and offended, but there have been a significant number who have come to me that were the offenders.

There is one couple in particular that stand out in my mind. Both the husband and wife were very talented and well educated people. They had beautiful, sweet children. All were in church, involved, and loved.

Everything looked well outwardly, but tragically the husband became involved with another married woman who was considered a friend to the family. The affair went on unknown for a number of months until suddenly it became revealed *(as sin always does – Numbers 32.23; I Corinthians 4.5; Luke 8.17; I Timothy 5.24; James 1.13-16)*.

The wife of the unfaithful husband was shattered and devastated (as were the husband and children of the other woman). Hurt that was unspeakably deep came in waves over the grieving wife.

What was she going to do? How was she going to make it through this raging storm and nightmare? God spoke to her heart. She knew that God wanted her to hold steady and believe for the healing and restoration of her home and marriage.

However, knowing what needed to be done and doing it seemed to be two different worlds swirling in two different orbits (which, in a sense, they were). The emotional pain was deep and almost unbearable. The mental images were grievous and mocking.

Not only was there pain, hurt, and anger toward the husband, but also toward the woman who had been considered a friend of the family. It was a brutally painful journey.

Before all of this became known the Lord had directed me to begin the series of messages on *The Dynamics of Forgiveness*. So while the affair was going on and after it became known this series of messages was in progress.

Conviction came (not only through this message series but through other messages, means, and people God used as well). Faith and repentance followed. Healing started. The marriage was restored through much counseling, love from friends, along with mentoring from strong men and women of God. Joy and laughter returned to the home.

But, this is not the end of the story. God never lets a tragedy be wasted when we put it in His hands.

A short time after this there was another marriage that was in peril on the other side of the nation. The wife in that marriage was a relative to this couple who had seen their marriage restored through forgiveness. The relative knew nothing of what had happened in the home of the couple whose testimony I just shared with you.

But this wife living on the other side of the nation one day picked up the phone, called, and talked to the lady who had seen God work miracles in her marriage through forgiveness (which was unknown at the time the phone call was made).

This grieving wife shared how that she accidently learned that her husband was having an affair via the internet with another woman in another state. This was a family of good means with children in the home. They had been in church at one time, but had become so busy with life, activities, and making a living they had stopped attending.

The wife who had seen God restore her marriage by pulling in closer to the Lord, believing while still grieving, going on with the Lord while day-by-day she was on an emotional roller coaster ride, began to share the power of God's love and forgiveness with her relative.

After the phone call this relative began attending church again with her husband and children joining her. And the God Who strengthened hearts and through forgiveness restored a marriage on one side of the nation now did it on the opposite side as well.

One of the beautiful outcomes from all the ugliness and hurt of an adulterous offense was how the lady from our church was blown away with how God could take her devastating tragedy and through forgiveness restore her home and marriage—and then use this tragedy turned to triumph to be instrumental in restoring yet another broken home and marriage.

What a powerful God it is Who reaches out to all of us in His love and grace. What a powerful grace forgiveness is that first begins with the Lord Himself coming into our lives through and by forgiveness. There are no limits to what God can do through forgiving and loving hearts!

"He comes alongside us when we go through hard times, and before you know it, he brings us alongside someone else who is going through hard times so that we can be there for that person just as God was there for us"

*(II Corinthians 1.4 The Message).*

# QUESTIONS

1. What are the two basic kinds of offenses in life?

2. Why do you think the problems of offenses and hurts are unavoidable in our lives?

3. What does the partial-knowledge problem speak to you of?

4. What are the three steps Jesus said we are to take in dealing with offenses in our lives caused by others?

5. In your words, how does forgiveness "bind" and "loose" in the light of what Jesus was speaking of in Matthew 18.18–35?

6. Why do you feel that forgiveness is really all that important to God?

7. Where is forgiveness to begin—and why?

8. Who and what do we acknowledge and give place to when forgive? How so?

9. In Thoughts what was the author's primary point of Forgiveness Releases Us to Minister to Others?

# Section Two

---

# FORGIVENESS: MAKING THE PROMISE WHOLE

---

# MARK 11.20-26 *(NKJV)*

²⁰ Now in the morning, as they passed by, they saw the fig tree dried up from the roots.

²¹ And Peter, remembering, said to Him, "Rabbi, look! The fig tree which You cursed has withered away." *(See Mark 11.12-14)*

²² So Jesus answered and said to them, "Have faith in God.

²³ "For assuredly, I say to you, whoever says to this mountain, 'Be removed and be cast into the sea,' and does not doubt in his heart, but believes that those things he says will be done, he will have whatever he says.

²⁴ "Therefore I say to you, whatever things you ask when you pray, believe that you receive *them*, and you will have *them*.

²⁵ "And whenever you stand praying, if you have anything against anyone, forgive him, that your Father in heaven may also forgive you your trespasses.

²⁶ "But if you do not forgive, neither will your Father in heaven forgive your trespasses."

# ALL, SOME, OR NONE!
## WHY AREN'T ALL OUR PRAYERS ANSWERED?

There can be those troubling and perplexing times and seasons when our prayers go unanswered because something is not right in our hearts due to offenses followed by the inevitable hurt, anger, and bitterness that in turn result in unforgiveness. There are numerous other reasons why prayers may not be answered, but those are not the scope of this book.

Offenses and unforgiveness can stand between us and the mountain-moving works of God in our lives and in the lives of our loved ones. Although, as just mentioned, this is not the only reason, it is, I believe, many more times than we may realize. The promises of answered prayer as set forth in Mark 11 involve forgiveness conditions that must be met and done. Unforgiveness arising from the hurts of offenses must be denied and put away.

> Right positions on issues bring us to right decisions; and right decisions bring us to the right places.

Right positions on issues bring us to right decisions; and right decisions bring us to the right places. And wrong positions lead to wrong decisions that will one day bring us to the wrong places.

This awareness was another part of the truth that I felt the Lord was revealing to my heart. This was what Jesus was saying to His disciples just outside of Jerusalem as recorded in our opening Scriptures of this section found in Mark 11.20–26.

How often, as we have previously discussed in the case of Matthew 18.18, we quote one of our Lord's promises in part without considering the entire whole of His words to us. Mark 11.23–24 is another one of those partial promise problems that we encounter in seeing answered prayer.

The problem with partial promises is that they only yield partial, if any, results. Like a spurt now and then versus a flow. And at other times the faucet is just totally turned off.

There is an old but true saying that illustrates this: "A **text** without a **context** is a **pretext**." That is, we must always consider what is said immediately before a verse of Scripture and immediately after a verse of Scripture *(which make up the context for the text)* to determine more accurately what that particular Scripture is truly saying and conveying to us.

> The problem with partial promises is that they only yield partial, if any, results.

This old saying would be illustrated by taking a Scripture from Judas' final earthly outcome from his betrayal of Christ:

"Then Judas...departed and went out and hanged himself" *(see Matthew 27.3-5 NKJV)*

and joining it with another Scripture from the Parable of the Good Samaritan:

"...Then Jesus said to him, 'Go and do likewise'" *(Luke 10.37 NKJV)*.

Taking these two texts out of their context and joining them together makes them a pretext which would read like this: *"Then Judas departed and went out and hanged himself. Then Jesus said, 'Go and do likewise'"*. A proposed 'truth' was created and even stated in words from the Scriptures that are not even remotely supported by the Scriptures themselves.

And this principle is true with the promises and directives of God in the Scriptures. We must keep them in their full context rather than picking a favorite part in one Scripture and then mixing it with another favorite part of yet another Scripture.

Jesus promised us that our words and prayers of faith would have dynamic results. They would curse and remove fruitless areas from our lives. They would move mountain obstacles from our way. The desires of our hearts would be fulfilled.

The only qualification that is overwhelmingly preached and taught from this passage of Scripture is that we must have faith and believe. Or, is this the only qualification? Look again at what Jesus says to us:

[22] So Jesus answered and said to them, **"Have faith in God.** [23] For assuredly, I say to you, whoever **says** to this mountain, 'Be removed and be cast into the sea,' and **does not doubt** in his heart, **but believes** that those things he **says** will be done, he will have whatever he **says**. [24] Therefore I say to you, whatever things you ask when you **pray, believe** that you receive them, and you will have them.

[25] **"AND** whenever you stand praying, **if** you have anything against anyone, **forgive** him, **that** your Father in heaven **may** also forgive you your trespasses. [26] But **if you do not forgive, neither will your Father in heaven forgive** your trespasses."
*(Mark 11.22–26 NKJV)*

Have you ever paid serious attention to the context of verses 25 and 26 when you were reading, speaking, or quoting in faith the promises of verses 23 and 24?

Notice that Jesus began verse 25 with the word "**AND**". This is what I am going to call *a divine conjunctive* word that ties-in, connects, and joins together in a relationship way the words spoken just before with what is said afterward.

"**AND**"! There was another qualification that Jesus was going to place upon mountain-moving, fruit-bearing, and desire-fulfilling words of spoken faith and prayer. Not only must we believe, but we must forgive where and when necessary as well!

Note also in verses 24 and 25 the word "**IF**" *(meaning "on condition that")* and the word "**FORGIVE**" *(a word of command and action)* that involves removing binding attitudes toward those who have offended us (whether intentionally or unintentionally, whether in actuality or just in our imaginations).

Then there are the words "**THAT**" and "**MAY**," which are *words of consequence* indicating the means of outcome and response on God's part.

So Jesus is telling us here that we must BELIEVE **AND** we must FORGIVE if we have anything against anyone to have a complete and full answer to and flow in our prayers. Actually forgiveness is a definite exercise of obedient faith as we shall see in Section 4 on What Forgiveness Is and Is Not.

When Jesus gave us the prayer model and the blueprint to build our prayer life with in Matthew 6.9–13 He told us in verse 12 to pray:

"And forgive us our debts, as we forgive our debtors" *(Matthew 6.12 NKJV)*.

This is the only part of that prayer model Jesus enlarged further upon when He said:

"For if you forgive men their trespasses, your heavenly Father will also forgive you. But if you do not forgive men their trespasses, neither will your Father forgive your trespasses" *(Matthew 6.14-15 NKJV)*.

As you consider these verses in Matthew 6 and Mark 11 compare it with what the Lord said through Isaiah the prophet about 700 years before Jesus' statements:

"Behold, the Lord's hand is not shortened, that it cannot save; neither his ear heavy, that it cannot hear. But your iniquities have separated between you and your God, and your sins have hidden his face from you, THAT he will NOT hear." *(Isaiah 59.1–2 NKJV)*

## It Is God's Will and Desire to Answer Your Prayers

THE **A-S-K** ACROSTIC (that I also write of in the Appendix of this book) assures us that God has a prayer providing, hearing, and answering heart.

[7] **A**sk, and it will be given to you; **S**eek, and you will find; **K**nock, and it will be opened to you. [8] For everyone who **A**sks receives, and he who **S**eeks finds, and to him who **K**nocks it will be opened. *(Matthew 7.7–8 NKJV)* [The letters made capitals, bold, and underlined by me are to emphasize the **A**sk-**S**eek-**K**nock acrostic]

Rest assured that every word of promise that our Lord Jesus Christ spoke will be fulfilled. All the promises of God find a positive yes and absolute affirmative fulfillment in Him *(II Corinthians 1.20).*

It is vitally important that we keep our prayer-line open and unstopped by sins of attitude that breed division, unforgiveness, and the like. Our marriage, home, and church can be greatly and gravely impacted by it as seen in the following Scriptures that imply offenses in the home.

"Husbands, love your wives [be affectionate and sympathetic with them] and do not be **harsh** or **bitter** or **resentful** toward them." *(Colossians 3.19 Amplified Bible)* **Bold** lettering done by author

"Husbands, likewise, dwell with them *[i.e., your wife -author's note]* with understanding, giving honor to the wife, as to the weaker vessel, and as being heirs together of the grace of life, **that your prayers may not be hindered.**" *(I Peter 3.7 NKJV)* **Bold** lettering done by the author for emphasis

If you are not seeing your prayers answered and the promises that you have claimed and spoken aloud fulfilled then take a closer look to be sure you are applying all to the situation and not just a part.

Be sure that you are not trespassing in regards to what is right in the sight of the Lord with bitterness, harshness, and resentfulness that always hangs out with unforgiveness, anger, hate, and the like.

It matters not how meticulous you build an automobile engine. Leave just one bearing or another part out and you will have only some of an engine and not a whole. If you get any response it will be partial at best, but it will not be the full response that is needed.

Jesus, in principle and effect, is telling us: Do you want to see my Father move in powerful and dynamic ways in your life? You want heaven to move on behalf of your family? Home? Marriage? Church? Do you want to see God do the exceedingly abundantly above all we can ask or think *(Ephesians 3.20)*? Then believe in your heart! Put your complete faith and confidence in God!

"**AND**," to make it complete and whole for Him to release His power flow that you are desiring to see work in your heart and life, if you have anything in your heart against anyone, then forgive and release it! Don't shorten your Father's hand and bind heaven's work in your life and in others by holding on to the sins of unforgiveness!

Jesus was saying through forgiveness we are to release the situation for the full answer. Loose the power of heaven to work. Let God arise *(Psalm 68.1; Numbers 10.35)* and have a free hand in the situation. Get out of the way. Turn it over to Him. As long as we are unforgiving we are binding the problem and answer. God cannot have a free hand. He cannot fully work. We will remain stopped from fully working by the hurts of offenses that we do not release through forgiveness.

It is God's desire and will that your church have a marvelous and mighty ministry in your community (and even beyond!).

It is the will of God that your home is happy, your family life blessed, and your marriage complete.

You are a member of the Body of Christ, His church. His body is to be alive and flowing *(see I Corinthians 12)*. Your home, marriage, and family come under a special provision of God's blessings and covering *(see I Corinthians 7.14)*. God wills and works to see that all of these things are filled with His bountifulness and goodness!

When you pray for an outpouring of the Holy Spirit upon your church, that is God's desire as well. You are not praying amiss. You are right on target.

When you pray for the blessings of heaven upon your life, home, family, or marriage, you are directly in line with the Lord's will.

When you pray for the salvation of loved ones and God's fullness for their lives you are completely Scriptural and in accord with the very heart of God Himself.

God hears those prayers. He works to bring all these things to pass. He has made every provision for each of these very areas of our lives—and more besides!

It is God's will that your entire family be saved *(Acts 16.31-34 & II Peter 3.9)*, your church triumphant now *(Matthew 16.18 & Ephesians 5.27)*, your life blessed, anointed, delivered, lifted, and receiving from the Throne of His Grace *(John 10.10, III John 1.2, Ephesians 3.14–21, & more)*.

Perhaps, at this point, you are saying to yourself, "I have prayed and prayed about these things, but little has happened. My prayers don't seem to get far above my head. Nothing appears to have changed. The mountains have not moved. The barren fig tree is still there. My desires are frustrated, not fulfilled. My church is dead. My Bible class is dwindling. I have no ministry ..."

Dear reader, Jesus' words never fail to be fulfilled in the life of every believing doer of them!

If a child who is ours and who we love is working to become a fulfilling and functioning person in life, there is nothing within our power or ability that we will not do to help them achieve!

As Jesus said, we don't give our children a stone in the place of bread, a serpent in the place of a fish, or a scorpion in the place of an egg. If this is true of we who are human parents, how much more so of our heavenly Father Who is love! *(cf. Matthew 7.7-11, Luke 11.11–13, and I John 4.16)*

God desires to do good things in our lives. If this were not so, then there would have been no purpose for Calvary, the resurrection, Christ manifested in human flesh, or any of the other many, many provisions that God has made available in Christ so He can do a good, full, and complete work in our lives.

The next time you are praying and all kinds of faith and expectancy come pouring forth from your heart, be sure to include verses 25 and 26 of Mark 11 in your qualifications list.

## FORGIVENESS IS ESSENTIAL TO ANSERED PRAYERS!

It is impossible for certain prayers to ever be fully answered until there is this loosening work of forgiveness exercised in obedience by a believing and praying heart.

God's desire and will from the time you were physically born into this world was for you to be saved. Even before! *(see Ephesians 1.4)*

Then why did it take so long for some of us to surrender our lives to Christ and be saved? The answer is simple.

It was not for a lack of God dealing with our hearts. If we think back we remember numerous times God reached out to us before we actually surrendered our hearts to Him. God worked. He convicted. He invited. But salvation did not become a reality in our lives until we believed, repented, surrendered, and received God's forgiveness.

It was not until the gift of forgiveness in Christ from God began to work in us that He was loosed in a manner of speaking to bring about the miracle of our new birth.

Again, unforgiveness binds heaven from fully working in our lives and forgiveness loosens heaven to work fully in our lives.

I am not saying that the only reason that prayers are not answered is because there is unforgiveness in our lives. There are definitely other factors that can hinder prayers (or, even seem to hinder) such as God's timing *(Revelation 6.9-11)*, our motivation *(James 4.3)*, insensitivity on our part to God's voice *(Matthew 13.14-15)*, and a number of other things.

However, I am definitely convinced from Scripture that many, many prayers are not being answered today and mighty works in some areas of our life are at a minimum due to unforgiveness and an alarming lack of knowledge of what real, Scriptural forgiveness is.

When we begin to harbor even little offenses in our hearts they begin to collect. And then over time there develops deadly toxins that are released in our spiritual nature. These toxins begin to spread through us unnoticed at first until deadly damage begins to manifest itself.

We become weak, spiritually lethargic, powerless, unable to effectively minister, pray, bless our marriage, home, and family.

If we have an unforgiving heart, then God cannot forgive us. And when there is unforgiven sin in our lives then it, in a real sense of thinking, short circuits our prayers and flow in the Lord.

More literally, it binds heaven from being able to fully bring about the needed answers and break-throughs in our lives. We look and see little to nothing because unforgiveness has closed the door.

When we allow ill-feelings in our heart and do not forgive, we bind ourselves along with the person or thing against which we are holding an unforgiven grievance, and we bind the Holy Spirit's full work in our lives! We bind and limit ourselves, others, and Him on earth and in heaven!

When we forgive, we release and loose ourselves, others, and the Holy Spirit to more fully work in heaven and on earth in and through us. Mountains move. Fig trees bear fruit and those that don't are cursed and removed. Desires are fulfilled. Mighty works and the wonders of God replace the miserable and mundane of littleness and nothingness.

And again I want to emphasize that forgiveness is just as essential for marriages, family, and homes as it is for our churches.

This is not only a must-truth for the church, but it is a must-truth for our homes, families, and marriages along with the many other vital and necessary life relationships as well.

In fact, this could very well be one of the most important truths that you will ever be made aware of concerning your marriage and family life. It could very well be of more value than anything you have discussed with a counselor.

Many, many marriages are suffering severe difficulties, even in the church, because husbands and wives are harboring unforgiveness against one another.

Many families are disintegrating due to the acid of numerous deep offenses and unforgiveness between the members of their family.

Again, unforgiveness binds the full work of the Holy Spirit. For many marriages and homes it is setting up division that will never be healed in any other way except through forgiveness. It has bound prayers prayed on behalf of the home and family.

There can be no real healthy bond, friendship, or fellowship in a marriage or family as well as in our churches until there is total forgiveness for anything and everything—and everyone!

Every hurt, every grievance, every annoyance has got to come under the cutting edge of forgiveness and be rooted out rather than plowed under where it can grow again at a later time.

I do not know what has happened in your particular home, or marriage, or life, or church. I do not know if detrimental things have been going on for you in these areas for a long time or a short time.

But I do know that regardless of the circumstances, the Holy Spirit cannot fully break through and move until there is a spirit of forgiveness that thoroughly sweeps through our hearts and through our lives.

I am not speaking of just learning to tolerate one another, or learning to live and put up with difficulties. You can learn to live with irritations and put up with things, but this is not forgiveness. It is not loosening heaven to work in the situation. You can learn to live in a bound situation, but you will see no mountain-moving works of God!

The situations will not be loosed until you learn to and then actually forgive. The full effectiveness of the Holy Spirit's work will not be seen until you forgive.

## OUR STRUGGLE WITH BEING TOLD WE ARE WRONG

The Holy Spirit is the only one that can truly and fully convict of sin and wrong. This is one of the important aspects of His ministry to our lives today *(John 16.7–11)*. Lasting awareness of wrong and sin comes from the work of conviction produced by the Holy Spirit in the depths of our heart.

For most of us it is exceedingly difficult for someone we love to correct us. We resent it. Even though the Scripture declares, *"Faithful are the wounds of a friend" (Proverbs 27.6)*, still we resent it.

It is only the Holy Spirit Himself working through someone or speaking directly to our hearts that can bring the conviction and full awareness of sin and wrong. Only then can offenses be solved, resolved, or dissolved through the ultimate work of forgiveness.

A humorous incident occurred that reminded me of how we struggle when another person tries to convince us of a wrong doing.

It happened one Sunday morning as I was preparing for the morning service at my pastorate when this truth of forgiveness was first beginning to enter and awaken in my heart.

I enjoy teaching as well as preaching, so I taught an adult Bible class during an earlier time in the Sunday morning hour. Time had slipped away as I worked on that morning message. The hour was late. I knew I had to leave by no later than 9:30 a.m. just to make it for the 9:45 a.m. teaching hour.

Finally I jumped up and announced to my family that I had to leave immediately. I told my wife to bring the other car and told my middle son, David, to go with his mother.

I was just slightly slower in getting around than I thought I would be so it worked out for my wife to ride with me in one car rather than taking two.

Our home, a condominium at that time, was a quad-level so David did not see his mother leave with me and go downstairs to our garage. We got into the car. My wife and I sat there waiting. No David. I honked. No one came. It was now 9:35 a.m.!

I jumped out of the car hurried through the garage and up the stairs to the house door. It was locked. The keys were in the car. I knocked. No answer. I pounded. No answer. I was exasperated.

I hurried back down to the car and got the keys. Just as I was starting back up the stairs the door opened and out came David nonchalantly (in those days he rarely got in a hurry).

I spoke to him, not as a preacher of the Gospel but as a frustrated father, and scolded him for keeping his mother and me waiting. I asked him didn't he realize that we that had to be an example to others!

He tried to talk but I had full control of the conversation and wasn't about to relinquish it.

I finished admonishing (scolding) him and we got into the car.

Finally I became quiet and David said, "Dad, I didn't know you were waiting for me. You told me to go with mom and I was waiting for her. No one told me you two were going together. I didn't see her leave with you."

Silence.

Then my wife, as only a wife can do, said to him, "Honey, forgive your dad. He just needs to pray a little more."

She was right! I was wrong! But, oh, I was offended and resented her telling me. Especially right at that time!

I sensed the Lord speak to my heart. "This is what I have been dealing with you about", He impressed to me. "You need a sensitive spirit and you need to release these things and frustrations to Me." Oh, my! Lord, forgive!

That did it. No more needed to be said. I was wrong, but could not resent it. I repented. I apologized. Only the Holy Spirit could so effectively and fully bring about this type of real, deep, and lasting awareness of the wrong I was doing to my home and son at that time.

Some years before this, when my wife and I began in the ministry shortly after we were married, I was very zealous for the Lord but, at times, without as much wisdom as needed at times.

In my mind I was among the elite few that had not bowed the knee to Baal *(I Kings 19.10, 14, and 18)*! The world was burning up and I was going to put out the fire! But, I had to be sure my own house was set in order first.

Very piously I set about to make sure that my wife had proper devotions each day. Day after day I would check up on her. Had she been reading the Bible as she should? Had she prayed properly and enough?

She very sweetly endured. For a while—a short while. Finally, enough was enough! She very humbly but firmly told me to back off. She reminded me that she had been serving the Lord long before I ever started and she had managed to serve the Lord all through her teens (a very commendable thing!).

Then she clinched it. She and the Lord, I was informed, were fully capable of keeping the fires of devotion and commitment burning without my constant badgering. In a word, you let the Lord take care of you and I will let the Lord take care of me in these areas of personal devotion.

Poor thing! Didn't she realize that I had the best of intentions and it was for her own good? Well, you can't help someone that's not willing.

"Lord", I finally said, "You will just have to take over and do what You can." I can picture the Lord shaking His head and smiling.

What a beautiful job the Lord has done—and is still doing!

She did not become apostate. An anointed ministry of music developed in her life that has blessed literally thousands of people down through the years of our journey together!

It was a valuable lesson to learn early in my Christian life. When I released her to the Lord He was more than capable of fully working in a full and unhindered way in both our lives. The Holy Spirit is able to do that which the Son has sent Him forth to do in our lives!

**Forgiveness is Letting Go and Letting God!**

## FORGIVENESS IS LETTING GO AND LETTING GOD!

Mountain moving works of God can only come as the Holy Spirit is loosed and not limited by us to do His work in our lives. Forgiveness is one of the major ways to loose the full working of the Holy Spirit in our life situations and relationships.

Forgiveness is releasing the "debts" that our spouse owes us, that our friends owe us, and that this and that person or even life itself, we feel, owes us!

When we harbor a "debt" against our loved ones, friends, leaders, and fellow workers we bind them and ourselves.

As we stand praying and releasing our faith, let us also release our brothers and sisters in Christ, that contrary sheep under our ministry, that offending shepherd, that offensive situation, that belligerent family member, so that heaven is not bound and limited but loose to work fully and bring about the desires of our heart and the needed change in all lives.

So many times when the Holy Spirit is doing the most tender and hidden works in our marriage, home, the life of our church or loved one in answer to our prayers, we barge in like the proverbial bull in a china closet when we have a heart of unforgiveness.

Many times, the Holy Spirit, with meticulous and loving care in answer to our prayers, has just started a work, a seed with miracle-working potential has been planted, roots of dynamic life that are unseen above the surface are just beginning to spread and we unaware trample all over the soil and harden it with the feet of unforgiveness!

The work is greatly hindered if not outright destroyed. The fig tree remains fruitless. The mountain gets bigger.

It is very important to realize that we cannot see the hearts of people. We cannot see the motives or the thoughts. We see only the outward signs, and many times they are far behind the inward work.

"...For the LORD does not see as man sees; for man looks at the outward appearance, but the LORD looks at the heart.'" *(1 Samuel 16:7 NKJV)*

In 1970 I had a history professor that stated: "It is not how things ARE, but how we THINK things ARE" that affects how we respond to the issues of life.

Far too many times our judgments are based upon how we think things are rather than how things really are. So much of our lives are spent in dealing with surface appearances rather than with the depths of realities below the surface.

> "It is not how things ARE, but how we THINK things ARE" that affects how we respond to the issues of life.

Only God truly knows it all. Only He is omniscient. Therefore we cannot afford to be unforgiving and thus bind and limit our eternal, omniscient Lord from being able to fully work in our life!

When we have a forgiving attitude, a tender heart and spirit, we will in effect say, "Lord, in the name of Jesus only you know this situation in its fullness. You alone can work this out for everyone's good. I forgive. I release them to you." Then the Holy Spirit is able to fully move. We loose Him, them, and us. The situation can then and will be worked out as we pray!

When I came to the Lord I wanted my middle brother to know Christ as his Savior too. I hounded him. I badgered him. At first he was very interested. But Cecil Barham just could not let the Holy Spirit do His work. I had to do it.

Finally in my desire for my brother to know the peace and joy I had found in the Lord, I rode him so much that he just wanted to be left alone. He went his way and I went mine.

A few years passed. He wanted nothing to do with my brand of Christianity. Then a tragedy occurred that almost emotionally destroyed his life. During desperate moments he walked into a pastor's office in Texas City, Texas, and wanted to know how to get saved. This pastor belonged to my church group of Christianity!

He surrendered his life to Christ as his Savior and, thanks to this godly pastor, was nurtured in the Lord. A few months later he was filled with the Holy Spirit. A year later he was called into the ministry.

He has since served in full time pastoral ministry, on church pastoral staffs as an associate minister, been a successful Christian business man, and is still active in a large ministry at his home church in the San Diego area.

The same is true of my youngest brother who served many years as a pastor and then as a state leader in his church movement in Oregon.

All the work of the Holy Spirit! When I got out of the way the Holy Spirit was able to do His work. We cannot nag or drag people into heaven. The Holy Spirit must draw them as their hearts are convicted of sin that leads to faith, repentance, and surrender to God's love and grace in our Lord Jesus Christ.

Reader, God can and will do the work and rain down His blessings in our life if we will let Him have the reigns of our life and circumstances!

There are mighty works of God awaiting you and your loved ones. Loose the ministry of the Miracle Worker by forgiving anything you might have against anyone. Bring your faith to bear upon those twisted relationships. Let God have them.

In the words of our Lord Jesus:

## "AND WHEN YOU STAND PRAYING, FORGIVE IF YOU HAVE ANYTHING AGAINST ANY."

# THOUGHTS

SINS OF LONG STANDING. There is a divine principle and truth that is found in the Scriptures concerning sins of long-standing that go un-repented of and thus unforgiven—on a national scale as well as for smaller groups and even individuals. As mentioned earlier in this book, God always gives a person, a church, a nation, and the like of what has come to be called **TIME AND SPACE OF GRACE** to correct sin, wrong, offenses, and the like in our lives through His mercy. Consider three Biblical incidents:

1. SAUL, THE FIRST KING OF ISRAEL in a misguided act of zeal for the Lord killed a group among the people of Israel known as the Gibeonites *(who were promised protection by the Israelites in a treaty some 200+ years earlier – see Joshua 9 & 10)*. This act by Israel's first king was never repented of by either him or Israel. Consequently a severe famine came upon the land many years later during the reign of the second king, David *(II Samuel 21.1–14)*. The Lord told David that he had to correct this long standing wrong. When David, as Israel's king, corrected the situation then God answered the prayers for rain and relief: *"...After that God heeded the prayer for the land."(II Samuel 21.14 NKJV)*

2. GOD PROMISED ABRAHAM AND HIS SEED (his descendents) THE INHERITANCE OF THE LAND OF PALESTINE. However, God told Abraham it would not happen in his lifetime *"...for the iniquity of the Amorites is not yet complete [full & complete –Amplified Bible]" Genesis 15.16 (NKJV)*. In other words, God was giving the Amorites **A TIME AND SPACE OF GRACE** to repent. When they reached a point of sinfulness that in time was so long and far-gone that they would not repent and turn to God, God judged them and gave the land to Abraham's seed, Israel. We speak more of this in our next section, Section Three.

3. ISRAEL'S NATIONAL SIN AND DAVID'S SIN OF FAITH IN NUMBERS RATHER THAN FAITH IN GOD

> Again the anger of the LORD was aroused against Israel, and He moved David against them to say, "Go, number Israel and Judah. *(II Samuel 24.1 NKJV)*

> Now Satan stood up against Israel, and moved David to number Israel. *(I Chronicles 21.1 NKJV)*

There was sin on a national level in Israel that was going un-repented of (unknown to us but known to them) and, in addition, David's heart was filled with pride in his army and his trust was turning from the Lord to the size of his military powers. God allowed, or, permitted Satan to use David's pride in numbering his army to deal with both David's sin and the national sin of Israel. David and the people had to repent and receive forgiveness.

4. THE SIN OF THE PROPHETESS JEZEBEL IN THE THYATIRA CHURCH.

> [18] "And to the angel of the church in Thyatira write, 'These things says the Son of God, who has eyes like a flame of fire, and His feet like fine brass: [19] I know your works, love, service, faith, and your patience; and *as* for your works, the last *are* more than the first. [20] Nevertheless I have a few things against you, because you allow that woman Jezebel, who calls herself a prophetess, to teach and seduce My servants to commit sexual immorality and eat things sacrificed to idols. [21] And I gave her **time to repent** of her sexual immorality, and she did not repent. [22] Indeed, I will cast her into a sickbed and those who commit adultery with her, unless they repent of their deeds.'" *(Revelation 2:19-22 NKJV)*

THE POINT. God will allow sin to go un-repented of for only so far and for so long before He brings in discipline and/or judgment. But even His discipline is designed for a set and limited time before He deals with the person, group, community, and/or nation in greater judgment. It is very foolish and unwise to waste the TIME AND SPACE OF GRACE that God gives us to repent of sins in our life so that discipline and/or judgment can be avoided or prevented.

# QUESTIONS

1. Do you believe it is God's will for you to pray and receive answers to your prayers?

2. If so, how do you know that it is God's will for you to pray and receive answers to your prayers?

3. Why are there prayers we pray that sometimes receive only partial or no answer?

4. Does forgiveness play an essential part in receiving answers to some of our specific prayers? If so, in what ways? Is unforgiveness the only reason for unanswered prayers?

5. What is the work the Holy Spirit does in making us aware of our sins called (what is the word)?

6. How important is the Holy Spirit's work in our lives?

7. What is the difference between how we think things are and how things really are?

8. In his Thoughts what is the author's primary point on Sins of Long Standing ?

# SECTION THREE

## EDIFICATION OR ERADICATION?

"The wise woman builds her house, But the foolish pulls it down with her hands."
*(Proverbs 14:1 NKJV)*

**EDIFICATION**: enlighten, inform, educate, instruct, improve, teach, build up

**ERADICATION**: remove, eliminate, get rid of, consume, wipe out, destroy, exterminate, do away with, stamp out, tear down

## GALATIANS 5.13–15 *(NKJV)*

[13] For you, brethren, have been called to liberty; only do not *use* liberty as an opportunity for the flesh, but through love serve one another.
[14] For all the law is fulfilled in one word, *even* in this: *"You shall love your neighbor as yourself."*
[15] But if you bite and devour one another, beware lest you be consumed by one another!

## GALATIANS 5.15 *(AMPLIFIED BIBLE)*

But if you bite and devour one another [in partisan strife], be careful that you [and your whole fellowship] are not consumed by one another.

## GALATIANS 6.1–2 *(NKJV)*

[1] Brethren, if a man is overtaken in any trespass, you who *are* spiritual restore such a one in a spirit of gentleness, considering yourself lest you also be tempted.
[2] Bear one another's burdens, and so fulfill the law of Christ.

# FORGIVENESS AS WE ARE NEARING AND ENTERING THE END-TIMES

As we move ever closer to the end-times as revealed in Biblical prophetic revelation there are dark forces of Satanic and demonic activities that are increasing with greater and greater intensity *(for information on what is meant by Satanic and demonic activity see the Appendix at the end of the book on The Satanic and the Demonic).*

These dark demonic forces are bent on the destruction and eradication of men and women, people of God, local churches, marriages, homes, families, God-fearing nations and people.

The Apostle John tells us that

"...the spirit of the Antichrist, which you have heard was coming, ... is now already in the world." *(I John 4.3 NKJV)*

For centuries now the spiritual forces of darkness that are not necessarily anti-religious, but are anti-Christ to their very core have been growing in greater dominion and influence in human hearts and minds. These malevolent spiritual beings see the approaching judgment and divine retribution foretold by God rapidly approaching and they are furiously working to destroy as many lives as they can.

One of the numerous tactics the spiritual forces of Satan are employing to destroy and eradicate is stated in Daniel as he prophetically speaks of the person who will be the Antichrist:

"He will **speak out against** the Most High and **wear down** the saints of the Highest One, and he will intend to make alterations in times and in law; and they will be given into his hand for a time, times, and half a time*." *(Daniel 7.25 NASB95)*

*i.e., 1 year + 2 years + ½ year = 3½ years—see and cf. with Daniel 12.7 and Revelation 11.2 "forty-two months", Revelation 12.6 "one thousand two hundred and sixty days" & verse 14 "a time and times and half a time", and Revelation 13.5 "forty-two months". This is the time length of The Great Tribulation, the last half of the 7 years of Tribulation just before the return of Christ to earth.

Satan is the master of distraction and deviation—and even more intensely so in the times we are now living. His chief tactic against the work of truth in our lives is deception as alluded to in Daniel where the Antichrist is foreshadowed and projected through the historical person of Antiochus Epiphanes:

[23] And in the latter time of their kingdom, when the transgressors have **reached their fullness**, a king shall arise, having fierce features, who **understands sinister schemes**. [24] His power shall be mighty, but not by his own power; he shall destroy fearfully, and shall prosper and thrive; he shall **destroy** the mighty, and also the holy people. [25] Through his cunning he shall cause **deceit to prosper** under his rule; and he **shall exalt himself** in his heart. He shall **destroy many in their prosperity**. He shall even **rise against the Prince of princes**; but he shall be broken without human means. *(Daniel 8.23–25 NKJV)*

I have consistently reminded my church congregations and those who have attended prophetic meetings I have taught that: Coming events always cast their shadows before them. And consequently those who live close to and just before their fulfillment see and experience the impact and effects of those shadows.

> **Coming events always cast their shadows before them.**

I believe from the many prophetic indicators that we now see happening in our nation and the world we are those living in the ever deepening shadows of these coming events.

Satanic/demonic forces will intensify their work of seeking to destroy and eradiate you, me, and others by isolating us with offenses, distractions, anxieties, pleasures, and the like so that we are alone and vulnerable to their deceitfulness of destruction.

Now is the time, as never before, when the local churches and Christian homes need and must be a place and people of refuge, renewing, encouragement, and strength to edify versus eradicating each other.

For this to be fully accomplished we must truly understand who our real enemy is—and it is **not** the Church, the Body of Christ, nor our brothers and sisters in Christ.

Jesus warns us of the spirit and mind-set that will be prevailing in the End-Times:

[10] "And then many will be **offended**, will **betray** one another, and will **hate** one another. [12] And because **lawlessness**\* will abound, the **love** of many will **grow cold**." *(Matthew 24.10 & 12 NKJV)* \*i.e., **living without God's Law**

Paul, in like manner, admonishes us concerning the End-Times:

¹ But know this, that in the last days perilous times will come:
² For men will be lovers of themselves, lovers of money, boasters, proud, blasphemers, disobedient to parents, unthankful, unholy,
³ unloving, **unforgiving**, slanderers, without self-control, brutal, despisers of good,
⁴ traitors, headstrong, haughty, lovers of pleasure rather than lovers of God,
⁵ having a form of godliness but denying its power. And from such people turn away! *(II Timothy 3.1-5 NKJV)*

Among the numerous coming waves of destruction and eradication in the very end times will be the slaughter and carnage of human life.

Revelation tells us that at one point up to one-fourth of all living people will die. In a short time following this, another one-third of those remaining will be destroyed. This indicates that approximately one-half of the entire population of earth will die within a few short years time *(See Revelation 6.7-8 and 9.18)*.

The dark demonic powers of Antichrist I am referring to are ultimately what is behind the horrific attacks on the Bible, Christianity, public prayers in the name of Jesus Christ, the ten commandments, and the like in our public institutions—even though all of these are an undeniable part of American history and heritage.

Satan knows that the Bible and prayer along with Christ-centered churches, marriages, and homes are what restrain and hold back deep and destructive sinful life-styles of immorality, sexual impurities, and violence that are bred by dark demonic forces.

What happens when these sinful life-styles and mind-sets arising out of the eradicating of the Bible in public life along with Christ centered praying, churches, and homes become the public norm? They further destroy the vitally important God-given relationships needed to preserve the unity in marriages, families, homes, and churches.

These spiritual forces of antichrist are producing a growing coldness of love and a deepening disregard for the sacredness of human life which is escalating now in our nation and the world.

We see it in the increase of mass killings in our schools and other public places, the destruction of our unborn innocents, and the attitudes toward the aging. And this is just the beginning of even more horrific things to follow.

When speaking of the end times and the carnage of human life Jesus stated:

"For then there will be great tribulation, such as has not been since the beginning of the world until this time, no, nor ever shall be. And unless those days were shortened no flesh would be saved; but for the elect's* sake those days will be shortened" *(Matthew 24.21-22 NKJV; cf. Daniel 12.1).* *i.e., the chosen

Praise the Lord, God assures all those who put their trust in Him,

"...When the enemy comes in like a flood, the Spirit of the LORD will lift up a standard against him." *(Isaiah 59.19 NKJV)*

And one of the primary means God uses to accomplish this is in His placing of prophetic anointings upon the ministry gifts of Christ to His Church *(Ephesians 4.4–16)* and imparting to the people of God timely truths that in the words of Jesus *"shall make you free" (John 8.31–32, 36)* from the deceitful and destructive tactics of Satan!

But we must become and remain vigilant while understanding the times we live in. The onslaught of darkness in this hour seeks to destroy and eradicate us individually by fragmenting our divinely appointed places of refuge and edification such as our churches, homes, families, and marriages.

This vital truth of forgiveness I am writing about is one of God's dynamic and effective weapons that will help us defeat this flood of destructive and eradicating darkness coming against our lives and against the vitally needed relationships of life found in Christ-centered churches, ministries, and homes.

## THE SACREDNESS AND VALUE OF ALL HUMAN LIFE

In these increasingly dark times that threaten to eradicate our lifeline relationships we must understand that forgiveness is as important in the eyes of God as human life itself is. This is a truth that you desperately need to hold to in the core and depth of your heart.

When you grasp this truth then the tremendous impact of how vital forgiveness is will grip your heart more so than ever before.

LOOK again at one of the most familiar and amazing Scriptures in the Bible. LISTEN to it. UNDERSTAND it.

"For God **so loved** the **world** that He **gave** His only begotten Son, that **whoever** believes in Him should **not perish** but have **everlasting life**." *(John 3.16 NKJV)*

This is far, far more than just a recital memory verse for boys and girls. It is a vital revelation from the depths of God's heart concerning his will and desire for every man, woman, boy, and girl from every tribe, tongue, creed, color, and race that is living, or, has lived, or, will live in this world! God's yearning in John 3.16 is reflected in another Scripture we considered earlier:

"The Lord is not slack concerning His promise, as some count slackness, but is **longsuffering** toward us, **not willing** that **any** should **perish** but that **all** should **come** to **repentance.**" *(II Peter 3.9 NKJV)*

Remember again the words of Jesus:

"Even so it is **not the will** of your Father who is in heaven that **one** of these little ones should **perish**" *(Matthew 18.14 NKJV).*

This means there is not one person ever born into this world that God's love manifested in the sacrificial atoning death of our Lord Jesus Christ was not meant for.

Not one person was born to be excluded from the offer of forgiveness in the work of Christ. EVERYONE is provided for. EVERYONE is loved.

It is heart breaking that not everyone avails themselves of God's love-forgiveness-provision in Christ that comes to every believing heart through the working of God's Word and Holy Spirit. It is heart breaking that not everyone will come in repentance to receive the Father's love provision of forgiveness.

It is as equally devastating that not every Christian and Church effectively realize how deeply God loves every person and that one of His primary reasons for giving us His Holy Spirit endowment of power was to take the message of salvation and forgiveness to every culture, nation, and person in the world.

What devastation it brings to so many lives when we as Christians fail to realize how much God yearns with love to save and restore because we have allowed our lives, churches, and homes to become fragmented as Satan seizes on our offenses and hurts as an opportunity to isolate us.

But when God's people do grasp this vital life honoring truth the whole spectrum of their thinking and purpose is revitalized and revamped resulting in churches and homes becoming whole again. And then this wholeness results in the saving of many lives through the healing flow of forgiveness in our vital relationship conflicts!

The Word of God is very plain concerning the attitude of God toward human life. All life is sacred in the eyes of God. The sacredness of life is what is right in the sight of the Lord and gives us that God-quality that in turn gives true meaning to life as we come to value lives as God does.

We were created in God's *"image"* and His *"likeness"* (see Genesis 1.26–27). All of us! All as in each and every man and each woman; each youth, each child, and each baby. The serious intensity of this is seen in what God said to Noah:

"Whoever sheds man's blood, by man his blood shall be shed; **for** in the image of God He made man." *(Genesis 9.6 NKJV)*

I do not recall anywhere in the Bible where you will find God commanding a man to be put to death for killing an animal, but you will find where God has commanded that any animal killing a man shall be put to death *(See Exodus 21.28–29. This does not in any way encourage cruelty to animals; e.g., see Proverbs 12.10 and Deuteronomy 25.4).*

The days immediately preceding The Flood were violent and wicked. Man was corrupt, and the imaginations of his heart were only evil continually until God was left with no other alternative than to destroy the corrupted people of that day *(Genesis 4-6).*

Only eight persons out of the entire world's population in that deteriorating time were found acceptable in the eyes of a holy God. And those eight happened to be one, God-fearing and honoring family—Noah and his wife, their three sons and their wives. This tells us a lot about how important a godly marriage, family, and home are.

Jesus said of the End-Times that

"And as it was in the days of Noah, so it will be also in the days of the Son of Man: They ate, they drank, they married wives, they were given in marriage, until the day that Noah entered the ark, and the flood came and destroyed them all. Likewise, as it was also in the days of Lot: They ate, they drank, they bought, they sold, they planted, they built; but on the day that Lot went out of Sodom it rained fire and brimstone from heaven and destroyed them all. Even so will it be in the day when the Son of Man is revealed." *(Luke 17.26-30 NKJV)*

The New Testament tells us that Noah was a

"PREACHER of righteousness" *(II Peter 2.5—and Lot who lived in another degenerate and evil time was said to be a "righteous man" II Peter 2.8)*

God waited as long as possible *(120 years!)* before bringing in the flood-waters of judgment *(Genesis, chapters 6 through 8)* and many years later during

Lot's day before raining down the fire of judgment on the cities and surrounding areas of Sodom and Gomorrah *(Genesis 19)*.

This means that God's heart of forgiveness reached out to both of those degenerate generations and called them to repentance and forgiveness.

The world of Noah's day died in the flood and those of Lot's day in the fire from heaven because its people were unwilling to repent from sin and turn to the forgiveness of God through grace—not because there was a lack of willingness on God's part to forgive.

God delayed judgment until He could do nothing else but destroy unrepentant people before they themselves destroyed <u>ALL</u> humanity through corruption and violence. Remember, there were only four marriages and families left in Noah's day that had restrained themselves from the corruption of their day and walked with God and only Lot and his two daughters alone in the communities of Sodom and Gomorrah.

After the Genesis Flood a man named Abraham was promised by God that he and his descendents would be given the land on the west and east sides of the Jordon River along with land well above the Sea of Galilee and below the Salt Sea to be theirs perpetually *(Genesis 13.14–17; 17.7–8 and approximately 150 other Scriptures)*.

As we noted earlier, at the time God made this promise to Abraham much of that land was inhabited by a people known as the Amorites. God told Abraham that this land would not become his nor his descendents until their fourth generation, as He said,

"FOR the iniquity of the Amorites is NOT YET COMPLETE" *(Genesis 15.16 NKJV)*.

In so many words God was saying He would not uproot nor destroy the Amorite people as long as there was a possibility of repentance and the opportunity for forgiveness to be extended.

It was not until the Amorites would become so totally degenerate in wickedness and in the destruction of human lives, and until there was no further possibility of their repenting of their wickedness, that God would bring in His judgment on their sins. And when that time came then God would give the land to Abraham and his descendents through the bloodline of his sons Isaac and Jacob/Israel *(Genesis 35.9–13)*.

Some four hundred years later when God was bringing that fourth generation of Abraham's descendents (Israel) out of Egypt under the leadership of Moses to possess the land He had promised to them, He gave them the Old Testament (Covenant) Law. You can read and meditate on it in Exodus 1 through Deuteronomy 34. And then consider that all of that vast Law is summed up in what Jesus calls the two greatest commandments:

First, "You shall love the Lord, your God, with all your heart, and with all your soul, and with all your mind, and with all your strength" and second, "You shall love your neighbor as yourself" *(Mark 12.29–31 NKJV; cf. Romans 13.8–10).*

Think back to the opening Scriptures of this section:

5.14 For all the law is fulfilled in one word, even in this: "You shall love your neighbor as yourself." 6.2 Bear one another's burdens, and so fulfill the law of Christ. *(Galatians 5.14 & 6.2 NKJV).*

You and I, Abraham and Amorites, and everyone else, are vitally important in the eyes of God. Consider carefully here the familiar words of our Lord Jesus:

34 "A new commandment I give to you, that **you love one another; as I have loved you**, that you also love one another. 35 By **this** all will know that you are My disciples, **if** you have **love** for one another." *(John 13.34-35 NKJV)*

Where there is love, there are forgiving hearts and spirits. Where there is forgiveness, there is the work of the Holy Spirit. Where there is the work of the Holy Spirit, there is understanding and enlightenment that edifies and builds us up so that we can truly see the Kingdom of God.

14 We know that we have passed from death to life, because we love the brethren. He who does not love his brother abides in death. 15 Whoever hates his brother is a murderer, and you know that no murderer has eternal life abiding in him. 16 By this we know love, because He laid down His life for us. And we also ought to lay down our lives for the brethren *(I John 3.14–16 NKJV).*

Where there is hate, there is unforgiveness. Where there is unforgiveness, sin and death reign in destruction and eradication!

20 If someone says, "I love God," and hates his brother, he is a liar; for he who does not love his brother whom he has seen, how can he love God whom he has not seen? 21 And this commandment we have from Him: that he who loves God *must* love his brother also. *(I John 4.20-21 NKJV)*

# IT IS GOD'S WILL THAT WE BE EDIFIERS

When we truly grasp the depth of God's compassion and desire He has for every person on earth we will become edifiers. Our churches, marriages, and homes will become places where people are built up versus being torn down.

Throughout the epistles of the New Testament, we are enjoined by God as His people to "edify", that is, "build up," the body of Christ, His church. We are to share one another's burdens. We are to receive and help the weak. We are to strengthen and encourage our spouse, children, home, and family.

Paul expresses this need of caring when he says:

> [11] And because of your knowledge shall the weak brother perish, for whom Christ died? [12] But when you thus sin against the brethren, and wound their weak conscience, you sin against Christ. [13] Therefore, if food makes my brother stumble, I will never again eat meat, lest I make my brother stumble. *(I Corinthians 8.11–13 NKJV)*

> [32] Give no offense, either to the Jews or to the Greeks or to the church of God, [33] just as I also please all men in all things, not seeking my own profit, but the profit of many, that they may be saved. *(I Corinthians 10.32-33 NKJV)*

These numerous Scriptures clearly reveal to us God is serious about the well being of every individual human being in the world, especially those in the Body of Christ, does it not?

If our heart does not cry with this feeling then is it little wonder that we do not even begin to comprehend and feel the urgency of how vital forgiveness is?

Until the revelation-depth of the John 3.16 truth and the like Scriptures of God's Word fill our hearts we will forever shrink in horror from Paul's words when he says:

> [1] "I tell the truth in Christ, I am not lying, my conscience also bearing me witness in the Holy Spirit, [2] that I have great sorrow and continual grief in my heart. [3] For I could wish that I myself were accursed* from Christ for my brethren, my countrymen according to the flesh." *(Romans 9.1–3 NKJV)*   *i.e., damned

If these words of Paul that he could wish himself damned if it meant that others might be saved seem too intense, remember, that is exactly what the Father gave His Son for and that is exactly why the Son came into this world! Jesus took our damnation (accursedness), our very wounds, bruises, chastisements, iniquities, and, some scholars believe, even our place in hell! *(See Isaiah 53.5–6 and Acts 2.31)*

Only the Holy Spirit pouring into our hearts God's love *(Romans 5.5)* and forgiveness could cause and move our heart to say this as Paul did (even though Paul clearly understood that only the sinless Son of God, our Lord Jesus Christ, could ever alone be the one who could take our sins and our place on the cross).

How many of us could honestly say that we would be willing to be damned if it meant the unsaved around us could be saved as a result?

How many of us would be willing to be damned if it meant that the one who has so grievously hurt us could be saved?

The tragic truth is this: We, for the most part at most times, are more willing to damn than to save—much less love and forgive!

Until the ministry of reconciliation *(see II Corinthians 5.18)* and the spirit of forgiveness penetrate our spiritual heart, we cannot understand the depths of love and forgiveness such as that expressed in John 3.16 and Romans 9.1–3.

> We, for the most part at most times, are more willing to damn than to save—much less love and forgive!

The heart and spirit of forgiveness longs to see men and women edified, not eradicated; built up, not destroyed.

There is no room in the heart of forgiveness for hate, bitterness, destructive wishes, and longings of revenge.

A heart of forgiveness cries for reconciliation and blessing instead of cursing no matter how many times people may beat you, imprison you, stone you, or lie about you. Consider everything that Paul suffered at the hands of others in the light of the statement about his willingness to be damned if it meant that others might be saved:

> [24] From the Jews five times I received forty stripes minus one. [25] Three times I was beaten with rods; once I was stoned; three times I was shipwrecked; a night and a day I have been in the deep; [26] in journeys often, in perils of waters, in perils of robbers, in perils of my own countrymen, in perils of the Gentiles, in perils in the city, in perils in the wilderness, in perils in the sea, in perils among false brethren; [27] in weariness and toil, in sleeplessness often, in hunger and thirst, in fastings often, in cold and nakedness— *(II Corinthians 11.24-27 NKJV)*

If Paul wanted to be vengeful, hateful, despiteful, ugly, bitter, hard, mean, and unforgiving, he certainly, according to our present world's view, had ample reason and opportunity. In the natural, people and life had dealt him many deliberate and horrible blows.

But Paul allowed himself by God's love to be lifted above all these things! The love of God flowed abundantly through his heart and life. His desire was for forgiveness, healing, and salvation, not revenge, destruction, and damnation! There is no fruit or gift of the Holy Spirit that specializes in destroying others or you.

*NOTE: Actually, Paul at one time was violent in his hatred and despising of all who called themselves followers of Christ **when** he was still Saul of Tarsus **before** becoming Paul the Apostle. And he did many of these very things such as beatings, imprisoning, death, and the like, to the church **before** Jesus transformed his life when he was traveling on the road to Damascus in his mission to hurt and destroy the lives of men and women in the church there (see Acts 7.54 – 9.3 and I Timothy 1.12–15).*

## Look Who's Crashing the Party

In Luke 7.36–50 of the New Testament we read of a dinner party of sorts that Jesus was invited to and had with a Pharisee by the name of Simon. If possible, it would be good if you could read that passage of Scripture at this point. If you cannot do so right now try to read it later. I will summarize and highlight it for you in the immediate following paragraphs.

From this passage of Scripture you discover that numerous people and guests were invited and were present for the dinner party this day at Simon's house. Jesus was there as his special guest when a woman, "who was a sinner" known in that city, showed up uninvited (and crashed the party as we would say today).

Simon, the Pharisee, knew the woman and from the implication of the narrative he had aught in his heart against her.

Simon's own sinful and unforgiving heart and spirit condemned [damned] her for who he thought she was. He also condemned Jesus for not knowing what *"manner"* of woman she was.

The truth of the matter is that Jesus truly and completely knew what manner of woman she was. It was Simon the Pharisee who did not really know. Simon only thought he knew. He knew in part when he thought in knew in whole. He saw her through a glass darkly when he thought he was seeing clearly. Recall here our earlier discussion in Section One on *The Partial-Knowledge Problem (I Corinthians 13.10-12).*

Simon was so locked in on the negatives of the woman that his unforgiving spirit could not see God's work of grace and forgiveness going on in her life.

Simon's unforgiving attitude locked in on this woman as a "sinner", a person of ill repute and unworthiness. He could see nothing else. Indeed, he would see nothing else. She was condemned in his eyes. There was no opportunity for fellowship. No opportunity for transformation.

Jesus' love and forgiving heart locked in on the woman's life. Forgiveness began to flow. Transformation transpired. Divine change took place. Love for God began to pour in and flow out from the woman's heart. Tears, love, and humility were born.

Simon's unforgiveness would have locked this woman into a life of bitterness, littleness, and hate similar to that of his own. His condemning, judgmental spirit defaced and devalued one that had been made in the image of God. One that was precious in God's sight. One that was included in John 3.16.

Jesus' forgiveness lifted her out of that village's streets of degradation, freed her from satanic slavery, caused a desert of human ruin to become a garden of God's creative beauty, and opened a person dead in darkness to the glorious light and life of God's redemption and liberty!

Jesus, the Son of God, **edified**. Simon, the Pharisee, sought to **eradicate**. Forgiveness always edifies. Unforgiveness always eradicates.

Forgiveness edifies churches, homes, families, marriages, friendships, neighborhoods, and communities. Forgiveness edifies our own lives because it provides an atmosphere in which the Holy Spirit can fully, freely, and creatively work.

Unforgiveness eradicates churches, homes, families, marriages, friendships, and people because it produces an environment of toxic poisons that destroy the needed responses to the Holy Spirit's full and creative works.

Forgiveness is the offspring of love, kindness, and tenderheartedness. Unforgiveness is the offspring of hate, hardness, and bitterness.

Forgiveness is of God and therefore brings life. Unforgiveness is of Satan and therefore brings death.

Forgiveness thrives in the atmosphere of the Holy Spirit and the Holy Spirit's mighty works thrive in the atmosphere of forgiveness. Therefore forgiveness edifies. It makes possible and builds up good relationships that could not have otherwise existed. Forgiveness

> Forgiveness is of God and therefore brings life. Unforgiveness is of Satan and therefore brings death.

channels God's graces into all of our interpersonal exchanges and relationships of everyday living.

Forgiveness reveres God's created image, man *(man is an all-inclusive term which includes both man and woman - Genesis 1.27).*

Forgiveness reaches out and embraces the un-loveable because, as it has been wisely said, those who deserve love the least need it the most.

> Those who deserve love the least need it the most.

Forgiveness is not a detachment from a person. God does not forgive us then detach Himself from us. Forgiveness makes it possible for God to become Immanuel in a personal way to us—God with and in us! Forgiveness brings us into fellowship and intimate friendship with God. Forgiveness brings good, godly attachment—not detachment.

Forgiveness opens the closed doors and possibilities to friendships and fellowships. It makes it possible for us to flow in harmony and ministry to and with one to another. It enables us to fulfill and be fulfilled.

Forgiveness edifies because it is of God. Don't be an eradicator and eventually wind-up eradicating yourself.

[13] For you, brethren, have been called to liberty; only do not use liberty as an opportunity for the flesh, but through love serve one another. [14] For all the law is fulfilled in one word, even in this: "You shall love your neighbor as yourself." [15] But if you bite and devour one another, beware lest you be consumed by one another! *(Galatians 5.13–15 NKJV)*

[1] Brethren, if a man is overtaken in any trespass, you who are spiritual restore such a one in a spirit of gentleness, considering yourself lest you also be tempted. [2] Bear one another's burdens, and so fulfill the law of Christ. *(Galatians 6.1–2 NKJV)*

## BE AN EDIFIER NOT AN ERADICATOR. BE FORGIVING BECAUSE YOU ARE FORGIVEN!

# Visual Aid: The Eye of Forgiveness

On the next page I have a simple visual aid placed in this Section Three of my book. This concept came suddenly and unexpected to me during a meal one day at the time these truths of forgiveness were first being opened in my heart and understanding.

The DARK CIRCLE in the very center represents the real and entire person that no one can fully see or know except God. A circle stands for that which cannot be wholly comprehended from one human point of viewing or seeing. The truth is we never fully come to know our companions of a life-time, much less the people we only come in contact with from time-to-time or on special occasions.

The PLUSES ( + ) represent the positive aspects of a person's life while the MINUSES ( – ) represent the negatives. The circumstances affecting our lives and how we have learned to deal with them will often determine how we are going to see and respond to a person, and how we are going to interpret other people's responses to us.

The primary point that laid hold of my heart is this: If we lock onto one or so negatives in a person's life, we can bind that entire personality in our mind and relationship with them to negatives. It may be a small minus or a large one. Accordingly it will affect our carnal mind and nature. Because the carnal nature itself is steeped in the negative of sin it will naturally be drawn and fascinated by the negatives in others. Water always seeks its own level *(for information on what is meant by the carnal nature see the Appendix at the end of the book on Background of Some Words and Phrases Used).*

An unforgiving heart and spirit will shut out most if not all other aspects of a person's personality and hold them for a lifetime to that negative in their life. When we lock onto a minus in a life the Holy Spirit is limited and does not have the opening at that point to transform the negative into a positive because there will be no prayers or endeavors to that effect by our unforgiving heart.

A forgiving heart will take into consideration as much as is humanly possible and then commit the entire whole, which is unknown to anyone except God, into His hands for correction, sanctification, and edification as may be needed.

**THE PLUSES (+)** represent the **POSITIVE AND GOOD** aspects of the person.
**THE MINUSES (–)** represent the **NEGATIVE AND BAD** aspects of the person.

God desires to change the minuses into pluses. This happens when we love and forgive. To see only the minuses is to lock that person into a Negative in our mind's eye and bind the work of the Holy Spirit in that area.

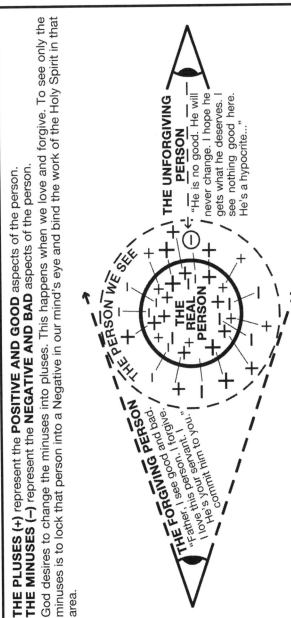

THE UNFORGIVING PERSON

"He is no good. He will never change. I hope he gets what he deserves. I see nothing good here. He's a hypocrite…"

THE PERSON WE SEE

THE REAL PERSON

THE FORGIVING PERSON

"Father, I see good. I forgive. I love this person. I love your servant. He's committed him to you."

**THE DARK-LINED INNER CIRCLE** represents the **REAL PERSON** no one but God sees.
**THE BROKEN-LINE OUTER CIRCLE** represents the **'PARTIAL' PERSON** we can see.

The circles themselves represent a wholeness that cannot be completely seen at any given time by any one person. We see only what is released from the real inner person. Potentials are there that can be seen only by the eye of love and forgiveness.

# THOUGHTS

1. **GENESIS 2.18** *(NKJV)* And the LORD God said, "*It is* not good that man should be alone; I will make him a helper comparable to him."

**PROVERBS 18.1** *(Amplified Bible)* HE WHO willfully separates *and* estranges himself [from God and man] seeks his own desire *and* pretext to break out against all wise *and* sound judgment.

**HEBREWS 10:24-25** *(NKJV)* [24] And let **us consider one another** in order to stir up love and good works, [25] not forsaking **the assembling** of ourselves **together,** as *is* the manner of some, but **exhorting *one another,*** and so much the more as you see the Day approaching.

**HEBREWS 3:13** *(NKJV)* but **exhort one another daily,** while it is called "*Today,*" **lest any of you** be hardened through the deceitfulness of sin.

**WHEN GOD CREATED MAN HE SAID, "LET US MAKE MAN IN OUR IMAGE"** *(Genesis 1.26)*. Man was made and designed NOT to be alone. God made the man and the woman and formed the marriage union that would result in the birth of children and thus form the home and family which in turn become the essential and crucial building blocks of all civilization.

As God continued to work in man he formed a God-centered bloodline, community, nation, and ultimately the Church (assembly). Godly people need other God-centered people to encourage, strengthen, uphold, love, and build-up (edify) each other. For this reason it is vital to our well-being to edify (build-up) one another by maintaining healthy marriages, homes, families, churches, communities, and the like.

The spiritual forces of darkness know this and seek to eradicate (tear down and destroy) marriages, homes, families, churches, communities, friendships, and the like by fragmenting, separating, and isolating us so that we are alone and vulnerable to the lies and deceitfulness of sin.

2. **GOD TEACHES US THAT FORGIVING ONE ANOTHER** is a dynamic and highly effective weapon that greatly aids in defeating the eradicating offenses that hurt us and can result in bitterness, hate, destructive anger, and unforgiveness. **When we forgive** we take away some of Satan's most effective weapons of eradication that he and his demonic hosts possesses to destroy us with.

3.  **DAVID WAS A MAN AFTER GOD'S OWN HEART** because he valued what God valued. King Saul unjustly turned on David to murder and eradicate him. But even when David had the opportunity to kill and eradicate Saul he instead chose to spare and honor him as God's anointed and leave his judgment in God's hands. The example of edification versus eradication is powerfully seen in this conflict between these two men chosen by God to be kings over Israel. It would be a blessing to you to read and reflect on it in I Samuel 13.1–14; chapters 15 through 26. Note chapters 24 and 26.

# QUESTIONS

1. What are some human behavioral signs of the end-times and the days leading up to it?

2. Is human life important in the eyes of God? And, if so, why?

3. What is the purpose of the design by dark spiritual forces to isolate people and to fragment the church, marriage, home, and friendships?

4. What do the dynamics of forgiveness do in helping us to be victorious in the dark days that are increasing around us which precede the end-time?

5. What are the primary differences between edification and eradication?

6. What is the author's visual aid on the Eye of Forgiveness and the Eye of Unforgiveness seeking to illustrate to the reader?

7. What does forgiveness do with the closed doors between us and other people that we come to know in our lives?

8. What does God's statement in Genesis 2.18 tell us about ourselves?

> And the Lord God said, "It is not good that man should be alone; I will make him a helper comparable to him." *(Genesis 2.18 NKJV).*

# Section Four

---

# WHAT FORGIVENESS IS—
# AND IS NOT

---

## COLOSSIANS 3.12–13 *(NKJV)*

[12] Therefore, as *the* elect of God, holy and beloved, put on tender mercies, kindness, humility of mind, meekness, long-suffering;
[13] BEARING WITH one another, and FORGIVING one another, if anyone has a complaint against another; EVEN AS Christ forgave you, SO YOU ALSO *MUST DO*.

## EPHESIANS 4.30–32 *(NKJV)*

[30] And DO NOT GRIEVE THE HOLY SPIRIT of God, by whom you were sealed for the day of redemption.
[31] Let ALL bitterness, wrath, anger, clamor, and evil speaking be put away from you, with ALL malice.
[32] AND be kind to one another, tenderhearted, FORGIVING one another, JUST AS God in Christ FORGAVE YOU.

## LUKE 23.34 *(NKJV)*

Then Jesus said, "Father, FORGIVE THEM, for they do not know what they do." And they divided His garments and cast lots.

# Understanding Some of the Various Dynamics of Forgiveness

The heart is staggered at the amount of unforgiveness that is in the hearts and lives of people today—and alarmingly this includes very many Christians. In our churches, marriages, homes, families, and our own lives.

As a result a real genuine and continuing outpouring of the Holy Spirit in our churches, homes, and lives is greatly hindered—and in some instances virtually non-existent in both inward and outward effect. There must be a definite turning in our hearts from a heart and spirit of unforgiveness that can lay deeply rooted within us.

Forgiveness is rooted in the nature of God's love. Unforgiveness in the human heart stemming from hurt, anger, hate, bitterness, and the like is satanic and rooted in sin's flesh-nature (carnal-nature).

A Scriptural understanding of forgiveness is needed for there to be a real, genuine turning from a spirit of unforgiveness. One of the primary purposes of this book is to help you arrive at an understanding of some of the important dynamics of what forgiveness is and the vital need to exercise it continually in our lives against offenses that would divide and isolate us.

The reason, in part, for this hindering condition of unforgiveness being of such great magnitude is due to our lack of understanding what forgiveness is in an overall sense of its nature. This was certainly true of me before that Saturday morning in 1975.

So I want to share with you the truths that I have come to know not only mentally but by actually living them out once I began understanding what the dynamics of forgiveness are and how they work in stopping the destructive offenses and hurts in our lives that stop us.

## The Varying Dynamics of Love

Let's begin by thinking about love. We find ourselves hard put to define what love is. The primary reason is because the Bible says,

"GOD IS LOVE" *(I John 4.8, 16)*

God is infinite and we are finite. It is impossible for the finite to define and completely understand the infinite. Therefore, real love because it is infinite eludes our finite definitions.

We can and do experience it by measures in our heart and spirit even though we cannot contain or grasp the fullness of its unlimited vastness to the point we can adequately define it in our minds.

Paul wanted the people of God, our Lord's Church, to experientially understand this infinite love of God. So he prayed:

"that Christ may dwell in your hearts through faith; that you being rooted and grounded in LOVE, [18] may be able to comprehend with all the saints what is the width and length and depth and height— [19] to know the LOVE of Christ WHICH PASSES KNOWLEDGE; that you may be FILLED with ALL the FULLNESS OF GOD" *(Ephesians 3.17–19 NKJV).*

Even though love is infinite and thus finitely indefinable, we still see quite clearly numerous and varying aspects of the dynamics of love because we experience them.

There is the dynamic of love that a husband and wife have for one another. There is the love that parents have for their children, and children for their parents. There is a love that a brother has for a brother or sister and vice-versa. There is a love that a friend has for a friend. There is a love that a Christian has for his Lord. There is that indefinable love that God has for His Own and even for an unregenerate world.

All of these varying aspects and dynamics of love in their stated relationships (and more that we could have mentioned) involve one thing—LOVE!

But, though each relationship has love in it, each has a distinct and different dynamic and aspect of love that is needed and appropriate for it. For example, to take the love that a husband and wife have for one another and try to apply that same love dynamic to any of the other mentioned relationships can be perverted and highly destructive.

Although each relationship involving love has a general tone *(such as that of I Corinthians 13)* the form of experience is different with each dynamic and aspect.
**So it is with FORGIVENESS.**

Our great problem is that we have basically and generally seen only one aspect or so of forgiveness and we have allowed that to define for us the whole.

Perhaps it would be more correct to say that we have only one or so concepts because most of us actually have not seen much forgiveness in any great degree or depth between one another!

## Two-Way and One-Way 'Street' Forgiveness

It is at this point, I believe the Lord has shown me something that, I feel, is going to be a great blessing to many that may struggle in the area of forgiveness. I would dare say that overwhelmingly most Christians have only the concept of forgiveness as a TWO WAY STREET.

That is, we see it as two people coming toward each other from opposite directions. The offender comes to the offended and says, "I'm sorry. I was wrong." The offended replies to the offender: "Oh, that's all right. It's fine. I forgive you. Let's be friends again."

Or, the offended comes to the offender and says: "You know you really hurt me...I am sorry for whatever I may have done to get you upset with me...but I want things to be right between us..."

Or, the offender and offended happen to run into each other after a period of time and they say to each other, "Hey man, you know, I'm really sorry about all of this." "Yeah, me too. Sorta silly wasn't it?" "Yeah. Wanna be friends again?" "Uh-huh." "Shake?" "Uh-huh." "All's forgiven?" "Yeah."

This may be over simplified, but it illustrates only one very small aspect of forgiveness. Forgiveness is not only a Two-Way Street but, many times it must be a ONE-WAY STREET!

The Two-Way Street aspect of forgiveness can definitely be very effective in the reconciliation between two persons or groups of persons.

However, what if there cannot be a Two-Way Street of forgiveness? For example, someone has deeply offended and hurt you, but that person is no longer living—although the deeds, words, hurt, and wounds are still living on in you via pain and memories? Or what if the offender never comes to you or will not allow you to come to them? Or the offender doesn't even know they have offended you and have long since relocated to a place you know not where?

My point is this: there may be many times and circumstances that you will have to forgive someone that has offended you without them ever being able to ask for it, or ever asking for it even though they are able. Or, even feeling they need to ask you for it.

You will have to do it alone many times for the simple fact that this may be the only way **you** will be able to get rid of that *"AUGHT against ANY" (Mark 11.25 KJV)* in **your** heart and loose **your** prayers so they can go through to an answer.

Actually, for the offended person, the One-Way Street of Forgiveness has numerous advantages over Two-Way Forgiveness. One-Way Forgiveness is not limited by time, place, space, moods, emotions, circumstances, personalities, or abilities.

Two-Way Forgiveness can only happen at certain times, when the involved persons are together or can make willing contact with one another, or when both are in the forgiveness-mood, or when each one has the ability to convey the proper words, tone, and the like that will not turn the situation into an even deeper offense.

One-Way Forgiveness needs only a willing heart to obey the teachings of our Lord Jesus Christ and it can happen anywhere at any time!

In fact, there are many circumstances in which Two-Way Forgiveness will never see forgiveness reached before we stand in the presence of our Lord for the simple reason it depends for the most part on the offender coming to the offended to ask for forgiveness, and that may never happen—or may not be possible to happen, such as in death!

Or, it may be, as it is in so many cases, that the offender is not even aware that he or she is an offender! This is due to the multi-facets of human nature and personality. A person says something that they meant in a kind or basically innocent way, but the person hearing it hears it in an unkind and malicious way.

How many times this happens! In our homes. Our marriages. During times of what we thought was *friendly* conversation. During a message intended to help and bless that is being preached in one of our church services. At a prayer meeting. Bible discussion. Ad infinitum!

I had a plaque once that stated the problem like this: *"I know you believe you understand what you think I said, but I am not sure you realize that what you heard is not what I meant."*

How painfully true this can be. And because it is true many offenses happen that no one knows about, but the person who has the aughts against the anys. Therefore, One-Way Forgiveness is the ONLY WAY that the aught-bearing person can loose the situation so God can work in their life!

Or, again as stated earlier, the offender may have died and is no longer available for forgiveness and reconciliation. It may be a more serious offense such as a parent who abused their child; a spouse who abused the other spouse; a business partner who cheated another business partner—and the list goes on and long.

The fact is that many, if not most, situations and relationships that must have the healing of forgiveness are of a private nature. There are numerous times when the offense is basically if not exclusively IN us. Many times it is HIDDEN there from the knowledge of other persons, including the offending party.

When we harbor hurt and hold our brother or sister, husband or wife, minister or layperson, or whoever or whatever, in debt to us we are actually sitting in judgment of them as we determine the amount of debt they owe us. This in itself can become a definite challenge to forgiveness.

And as I continue to emphasize, compounding the complexity of the situation is that we are so many times the only ones (except for God!) that know this is happening.

We must, in these circumstances, act in One-Way Forgiveness and before God's Throne of Grace release them from our judgment and forgive! We must say, "I am not capable of judging this one. I do not truly know everything in their heart. I do not really know all their motives. Lord, this belongs to You and You alone. I release them to you. I cancel the debt I feel is owed to me. I forgive them."

The Scriptures tell us, *"Do not grieve the Holy Spirit"*, and the verses following clearly show us that harboring an unforgiving spirit is one of the things that grieves the Holy Spirit Himself.

> [30] And DO NOT GRIEVE THE HOLY SPIRIT of God, by whom you were sealed for the day of redemption. [31] Let ALL bitterness, wrath, anger, clamor, and evil speaking be put away from you, with ALL malice. [32] AND be kind to one another, tenderhearted, FORGIVING one another, JUST AS God in Christ FORGAVE YOU. *(Ephesians 4.30–32 NKJV)*

When the Holy Spirit is grieving He cannot bless nor work in fullness in our life or situation. And unforgiveness grieves Him because it binds and limits Him so that He cannot flow in our lives and impart the heart of Christ to us.

Revival will not come nor continue where the Holy Spirit is grieving. Marriages will not have the fullness of God's blessings upon them where the Holy Spirit is grieving. Churches will not flow with or in the presence of God where the Holy Spirit is grieving.

There may be *mercy-drops* but, there will be no showers or outpourings. So many times God's *mercy-drops* are the *tear-drops* of the grieving Spirit of God in goodness calling us to repentance! *(cf. Romans 2.4)*

A Spirit-filled life and walk that honors God's Word along with revering God Himself is an absolute essential to fullness and completeness in our Christian experience. This fullness in our Christian experience is an absolute essential to completeness in our homes, marriage, churches, and interpersonal relationships of everyday life.

> So many times God's *mercy-drops* are the *tear-drops* of the grieving Spirit of God in goodness calling us to repentance!

This unlimited fullness does not come without forgiveness! All forgiveness. Whether Two–Way Forgiveness, or One–Way Forgiveness.

## A PRACTICAL OBSERVATION

I am going to deviate a little from our present consideration of forgiveness to sound a word of caution at this point.

Do not feel that you have to approach everyone you feel ought in your heart against to confess and apologize. In most cases this should be done only when the offense is known by both persons or parties.

I remember quite vividly in one of my pastorates a time when God was moving greatly in the hearts of the people. In one of the Sunday morning services where several hundred people had gathered there was such a genuine move of the Holy Spirit that people stood and publicly began confessing wrongs, aughts, and unforgiveness that they had held against one another for over twenty years! How God loosed that church and those lives.

This continued for a number of weeks and once this began and continued many wanted to be free from unforgiveness. Some in their zeal went to people and began to confess things that only they themselves knew they held aughts over.

One young lady with a very vibrant and outgoing personality, who was among our newer converts, had about five or so people come to her with confessions and apologies. She never dreamed any of these people felt negatively toward her. For a while it almost devastated her.

Finally she came to me and asked: "Pastor Barham, am I really all that bad? What in the world is wrong with me? I never realized what a bad person I must be to have offended that many people!"

It would have been far better for those five or so people to have taken the things they were feeling toward that young lady before God's Throne of Grace in One-Way-Forgiveness.

We must be careful. Proceed Scripturally and Spirit-led. The rest you can do privately with just you and the Lord. After all, you and He are the only ones in many instances that know the aught is there, so you and the Lord can work it out.

If you feel that you must say something to the individual that you have felt aught against do it AFTER you have thoroughly loosed the situation in One-Way Forgiveness. Then go to them, and rather than mentioning the specific offense (because it is all under the blood now), tell them how much you love them in the Lord! That will work wonders for everyone.

Now let's look at what forgiveness IS and IS NOT.

## FORGIVENESS IS NOT THE LOSS OF FEELING— IT IS THE LOOSING OF FAITH

We will illustrate this from a Scripture that deals with another aspect of the Christian life. The Word of God instructs and counsels us,

"in everything GIVE thanks; for this is the will of God in Christ Jesus for you"
*(I Thessalonians 5.18 NKJV)*

For years I used and quoted this scripture in various messages I preached. However, one day I came to realize that I had been quoting and saying the right words, but I had been unconsciously reading another word into one of the key words in that scripture.

I was actually, in my mind, reading that verse to say: *"In everything FEEL thanks"*. The day came, thank the Lord, when the Lord's inward still, small voice corrected me. God did not say to FEEL thankful in EVERYTHING, but to GIVE thanks in EVERYTHING! This is part of what is meant by the *"SACRIFICE of praise" (Hebrews 13.15)*.

What a glorious difference this was! What a heavy burden of struggle this lifted from my life. It is far more possible and workable to GIVE thanks in faith because *"all things work together for good" (Romans 8.28)* than to FEEL it—especially at certain times! Plus it is Scriptural and releases divine power to work in our lives. It was a counsel and command of FAITH, not FEELING, as are all the promises and commands of God.

And this is true of all the grace possessions of our Christian life coming through the atoning blood and work of Christ in His crucifixion, resurrection, and ascension.

I am not SAVED because I FEEL saved. I am saved because God SAID I was and I put my FAITH in what He says and BELIEVE it! FEELINGS do not save me. FEELINGS are not salvation. Thank God for the feelings OF salvation but, praise the Lord, feelings are NOT salvation.

> Thank God for the feelings OF salvation but, praise the Lord, feelings are NOT salvation.

"And this is the victory that has overcome the world—OUR FAITH" *(I John 5.4 NKJV)*

It is not what I FEEL; it is putting my FAITH in and accepting what God says about Jesus Christ in my life that overcomes the world and is the victory!

This same basic principle is true of forgiveness as well. Fulfilling the commands and promises of forgiveness are obedient responses of FAITH, not FEELINGS!

FEELINGS are NOT FORGIVENESS. It is very possible for the feelings of hurt, disappointment, being crushed, disillusionment, and such to linger, flow and ebb on and off for sometime AFTER the obedient and dynamic faith steps in forgiveness have already taken place.

Most of us have confused feelings with forgiveness (as we have done in so many other areas of our Christian life). We attempt to forgive, but when the feelings of hurt, disappointment, and such linger on, the enemy deceives us into thinking that we have not really, truly forgiven after all or we would not still be having these feelings.

The truth is that the needed healing from these destructive feelings cannot take place until we by obediently in faith forgiving loose the Holy Spirit to work on and in them. When we step out in faith and forgive, the Holy Spirit immediately begins to work in our lives and in the lives of those that we are forgiving!

We begin to be loosed from the destructive feelings that fester and poison in an unforgiving heart the moment we in obedient faith begin to forgive. The fruitless fig tree of unforgiveness begins THEN to dry up from the roots! The mountain obstacles standing between us and our full fellowship in the Lord and His power begin THEN to be moved!

In Step Five of Forgiveness we will look some more at understanding what is going on with the reoccurring feelings of hurt, bitterness, and the like that we may experience after we have stepped out in faith to forgive.

## FORGIVENESS IS FORGING NEW MEMORIES — NOT FORGETTING OLD ONES

Yes, I am very much aware of the old saying, "You must forgive and forget." How many times I have preached it from my pulpits, said it to family and church members, and even applied it to myself!

What a shock it was when the Holy Spirit began to do a work of forgiveness in my own life during the days immediately following that Saturday in 1975 and He began revealing things to me that I had FORGOTTEN, but never FORGIVEN!

When I say "forgotten" I mean things were no longer in the fore front of my conscious mind, but had slipped into the debris and clutter of what many now call the subconscious mind.

We actually NEVER FORGET ANYTHING. Things are locked permanently into our brain as long as the brain is intact. They lay there awaiting the stimulus that will produce recall (i.e., conscious memory or remembering).

Many times these things in our subconscious level are still at work producing very definite effects in our lives that we can't quite put our finger on.

The brain stores everything and then under the proper conditions and stimulus recalls it to the fore front of consciousness again. In other words—we remember.

You may have heard of the PHANTOM-LIMB EXPERIENCE. This is when someone has had a hand, foot or such completely severed or amputated. For years after such a loss there are amputees who tell of still FEELING that limb at times even though it is no longer attached to their body. They still FEEL the pain even though the area and cause of the pain have been removed long ago.

Why? Because our nervous system still has the MEMORY of that limb, the pain, the itch, and the like even though they are no longer there.

It is similar with forgiveness. We can, so to speak, amputate or sever with the Sword of the Spirit (God's Word) those destructive attitudes and intentions from our lives by forgiveness, but the memory of them will at times be recalled.

As I wrote earlier, what a shock it was when the Holy Spirit took me on a journey into the deeper recesses of my heart and showed me things, persons, and places of many years standing that I had supposedly forgotten, but not forgiven.

I had always prided myself in being able to keep hurt feelings, bitterness, and the like from taking hold of my outward life because I had witnessed the terrible destruction that occurs from them.

In my pride I had always pictured myself as a person who could roll with the punches. Pride, being the number one of the seven greatest sins, is never good for any person, marriage, church, or the like.

But, there they were. I had not forgiven and forgotten. I had only put them out of my sight. They were still there. And from time to time they would creep out and short-circuit the flow of the Holy Spirit in my life and then quickly scurry away back down into the dark recesses of my heart before I could recognize and understand why the flow had been interrupted.

Out of sight, out of mind!

No. Out of sight but, not out of mind. They are still there. Hiding. Waiting.

I repeat. It is impossible to forget anything (unless that area of the brain is destroyed by something such as a stroke, disease, accident, or the like).

Once this brain of ours that God has designed hears something, sees it, tastes it, feels it, or smells it with any of the five primary physical senses, it is stored in a memory bank like a computer awaiting the proper input to be recalled.

Here is what I feel is a very vital and important truth about the process of forgiveness. When we forgive, we literally start taking the needed steps to OVERWHELM THE OLD MEMORIES of hurt, pain, disappointment, and the like WITH NEW MEMORIES of forgiveness, release, power, and deliverance. This way when the old memory is recalled (remembered) so is the new memory. After awhile the domination of the memory of hurt gives way to the memory of healing.

In the fourth chapter of Joshua, in the Old Testament, we read how the Lord commanded Israel to set up twelve stones from the midst of the overflowing Jordan River when they passed over from the east shore to the west shore of the Promised Land dry-shod as a result of the miraculous working of God.

The stones were large and heavy. They would have to be in order to endure through the years as a memorial marker. It does not take any stretch of the imagination to know that the men who carried those large stones would long remember the weight, toil, cuts, pain, and energy required to transport them via their own muscles.

However, the memory of the toil and pain would immediately give way to the other memory of the miraculous crossing and wonder working power of their God. The stones would remind them of the ENTIRE occasion and accomplishments of that awesome day. The memory of the toil, strain, and even pain were overcome by the memory of the awe, the miraculous, the power, and the impossible that God worked that day for His people.

The MEMORIES OF FORGIVENESS become our STONES OF MEMORIAL of the work of God in the situation that had confronted us with deep pain and agony. We remember the marvelous. We remember the Lord holding back a raging river of passions and attitudes that would not let us cross over and possess the Lord's Promised Land for us. They become memories of joy unspeakable at God working His mighty healings in the depth of our spirit and soul.

Experiences that are deep and impacting leave a lasting impression on our minds and memory whether they are experiences of pain or pleasure.

Memories of pain must be overwhelmed and flooded with new and deep experiences of God's work of forgiving power and pleasure. This is what happens when we forgive! We begin overwhelming death with life. Both will be there, but the negative will always be overwhelmed by the positive. That which once brought us down into the depths will now lift us into heavenly places.

After you have forgiven, you can count on Satan bringing back the memory of the old hurt—but with it now comes the memory of healing. We begin to rejoice. The devil's tactic is emptied of its power of distraction and doubt!

He will now do his best to see that he does nothing to stir up either of these memories!

When we remember something it is literally recalled to the conscious forefront of our minds. We then hold it before our self.

Remembering is an action word. It can happen by hearing a key word, seeing a picture or object (such as a certain gift a person at one time gave to you), the sound of a song that recalls an occasion, a certain smell of a perfume or cologne or a meal our mother cooked, or numerous other things that trigger in us a recalling of something that we then begin thinking on.

Remembering can be a time when we willingly allow certain destructive thoughts—ones we may be struggling with forgiveness over—to remain on the center stage of our minds.

Unfortunately so many times it is the bitter and ugly things of our lives, homes, marriages, and churches that we allow to dominate and occupy the forefronts of our minds.

We dwell on them. Thinking about them is like hitting and putting pressure on an infected sore. It intensifies the pain in our system. It destroys or slows the healing process at work. The wound cannot heal.

The one vital thing we need God to do now is to give us new experiences of spiritual healing. When we forgive, this is what is happening. God brings in new memories, new experiences, that begin to literally overwhelm the old.

Yes, you will remember the old. But just as you remember the old, you will also remember the new work of the Lord in your life. There will be new and better key words, songs, and heavenly fragrances that will call forth memories. Where a memory used to bring a scowl across your face and filled your heart with remorse and bitterness it will now bring a smile as you remember getting down before the Lord and loosing and releasing the situation through forgiveness into His hands.

Instead of a negative memory it becomes a beautiful memorial to the grace of God and the work of the Holy Spirit in your heart and life. We are wise when we stay focused on what God is doing through forgiveness in our life. When we focus on the healing rather than the hurt.

## FORGIVENESS IS FORGING A RIGHT RELATIONSHIP— NOT A FORM OR A RITUAL

We picture forgiveness as an exchange of apologies such as we were writing of earlier in this chapter. But forgiveness is far more than an outward motion of emotions coupled with the exchange of certain words.

Forgiveness is in reality a state of our heart and mind. It is the forging of a right relationship with the Lord. It is a right spirit. It is an inward disposition of Christian character made up of the Fruit of the Spirit.

Go back to the beginning of this chapter and read again very carefully the Scriptures we have given you. Better yet, if possible, go to your Bible and read them in their entire context. Then compare them with the Fruit of the Spirit given in Galatians 5.22–23. This is the reason why I said that forgiveness is an inward disposition of Christian character made up of the Fruit of the Spirit— and this fruit can only come as we WALK in the Spirit of God!

Try starting your day with the Lord's Prayer *(Matthew 6.9-13)*. When you come to *"And forgive us our debts, as we forgive our debtors"* picture yourself putting on the mind, heart, and spirit of forgiveness and going forth that day to forgive any and all offenses that may come against you.

You and I are literally to be the vehicles of God's mercy and grace. We are to be forgiveness on the way to being dispensed where and when needed.

We are to be peacemakers and mercy-givers. Not a portable courtroom with a one man package of judge and jury! We have been sent to loose good, not to bind it. We have been sent to set the captives free not to imprison them again! *(Luke 4.18–19)*

Probably by now you have noticed that as we have been showing you what forgiveness is not, we were also contrasting it with what forgiveness is.

This is natural and a necessary part of the learning process. We understand what tall is because we understand what short is. We understand what loud is because we understand what quiet is. We understand what black is because we understand what white is.

We begin to better understand what forgiveness is when we begin to understand what forgiveness is not.

Forgiveness is laying to rest the past by walking with Christ in the present. It is determining that you are not going to let the past bind or define you. You are going to be loosed from the past to serve Christ unhindered in the present as you journey into your future!

Here is a little food for thought. Jesus said,

> **Forgiveness is laying to rest the past by walking with Christ in the present.**

[23] "But the hour is coming, and now is, when the true worshipers will **worship** the Father **in spirit and truth**; for the Father is seeking such to worship Him. [24] **God is Spirit**, and those who **worship Him MUST worship in spirit and truth**" *(John 4.23–24 NKJV)*.

There is another word that can be used for truth. It is the word **reality. Truth is reality and reality is truth**. A lie is basically a non-reality (or, at best, a distorted-reality).

Yesterday WAS a reality, but it is no longer a reality but a memory of reality! Today IS reality. The present IS reality. Therefore, in a very unique sense, we must be CURRENT in our worship of the Father. We must be IN THE PRESENT and not just in the past. It WAS wonderful to be in the Spirit yesterday (or, in the past) but, we *"MUST"* be in the Spirit today as well!

What a tragedy to let what we had or what happened yesterday take away what is ours in the Lord today, or to throw away what we have today for a to-morrow we may never have. I could expand on this further, but I believe this is sufficient to understand what I am saying.

The tragedy of letting the past fill our lives is that it allows limited, little, or no room for the present. The Scriptures declare that God

"DAILY loads us *with benefits"* (Psalms 68.19 NKJV), and He told us to pray "Give us THIS DAY our DAILY bread" (Matthew 6.11 NKJV), and that "This is the DAY the LORD has made; We will rejoice and be glad in it." (Psalm 118.24 NKJV).

EVERYDAY God is active, moving, working, revealing, advancing, and speaking. We must stop letting the hurts and offenses of the past stop us from living in God's healing and overcoming power today.

To harbor things of the past, especially hurt feelings of offensive things, is to leave little or no room for the new and the fresh blessing and word of God in us today.

FORGIVENESS IS putting the offensive hurts of yesterday under the blood of our Lord Jesus Christ and reaching forth to receive today the fresh and new coming from the vast storehouses of our Father's riches in His Son.

Why let some past crossword, some past detrimental act, some past ugly situation, keep us from the power of His Word, the uplifting work of the Holy Spirit, and the beauty of His Person filling our lives NOW TODAY!

Did you know that you can bind your pastor from ministering to you the riches of Christ NOW by unforgiveness? If a church is holding PAST things against its shepherd it binds that shepherd from ministering and leading NOW in their lives.

When you forgive your pastor you loose him to minister to you NOW and you loose him to the work of the Holy Spirit in his own life.

A pastor can feel when his people are loosening him to minister or binding him!

By the same token the pastor can bind his congregation from receiving from his ministry and in turn strengthening his ministry if he is unforgiving. A pastor can loose his congregation by forgiving.

Put the past behind you. Reach out and live in the present. Forgive!

We think we know so much about everyone when we have been in a church for any period of time, or, when we have been married to our spouse for a number of years.

Without realizing it, we will live constantly with them in the present filled with what has been done by them in the past if we do not have a forgiving heart.

This, in part, is what happened to the people of Nazareth concerning their attitude and offense toward Jesus. They could not on that day recorded in Matthew 13.54-58 see Him standing there as their Messiah because they were so filled in their minds and hearts with his past as just a carpenter, as just one boy among other brothers and sisters that grew up in the old hometown *(also recorded in Mark 6.1–6 and Luke 4.14–24)*. And they were offended by what He was saying to them and doing in their midst.

If this is true of the One who never had sin, how much more is it true of we who have made our share of bad judgments, mistakes, and the like? No wonder the Body of Christ in so many local churches is bound!

You will be amazed at what God can do in an atmosphere of forgiveness. When there is forgiveness filling a church, a home, a marriage, and the like there is going to be continuous workings of the Holy Spirit. When by forgiveness you loose yourself and your friends in Christ from the PAST God will be able to move NOW in the PRESENT!

Forgiveness is turning away from revenge and vengeance. It is not, as we have pointed out earlier in the book, turning people over to God hoping that He will do them in good and proper for you. It is stepping out of the way and saying, "Lord, I want nothing more to do with judging these people. I am not capable of it. Lord, you correct the situation. Get glory from it. Defeat Satan in this."

Forgiveness is releasing your soul from the attitude and thoughts of revenge, bitterness, and hate. It is, in a very beautiful sense, the continuation of the Lord's atonement through our lives—or at-one-ment as it sometimes expressed with a play on the word. It is God's grace. It is kindness and tenderheartedness working through us to others. It is the very Word of God bound in the very best leather binding a Bible can have—our shoe leather.

Forgiveness is not just saying, "I love God." It IS loving God. *(I John 4.20—see the entire book of I John!)*. Forgiveness is not just SAYING, "Lord, I will serve you." It IS serving the Lord! *(James 2.14–18)*

Forgiveness is not just saying, "Lord, I believe your Word." It is BE-<u>LIVING</u> His Word (I did not misspell believing but purposely used the word living). His Word said,

"And BE kind to one another, tenderhearted, FORGIVING one another, JUST AS God in Christ FORGAVE YOU" *(Ephesians 4.32 NKJV)*.

Again, forgiveness is an attitude, disposition, and state-of-being that deals not only with people, but with things, situations and even life itself!

There are people filled with bitterness at what they feel is their lousy lot in life. The number one hit song of their life is, "Born to Lose". The Word of God unequivocally declares,

"Whatever is born of God OVERCOMES the world" *(I John 5.4 NKJV)*

You will be overjoyed at how far an attitude of forgiveness will go toward curing a sour disposition over the miseries of life!

Many of us might be shocked when the Holy Spirit begins to show how we have carried an unforgiving attitude toward our parents, grandparents, and perhaps even our great-grandparents. We think, "If they had just been on the ball...a little smarter...more diligent...they could have been rich and left me with a good inheritance like others I have heard about. You didn't leave me anything...why couldn't I have been born into some other family besides yours...!"

These are thoughts and attitudes that defeat us and limit the Lord's work in and through our lives. Forgiveness looses us from these and like issues to walk in our Father's provisions for our lives. Forgiveness is freedom from things that bind us to walk in that which blesses us.

> Forgiveness is freedom from things that bind us to walk in that which blesses us.

# WITH ALL OF THESE THINGS IN MIND TAKE A FRESH LOOK AT THE LIFE OF JOSEPH

## (SEE GENESIS 37 – 50 * ALMOST 1/4ᵀᴴ OF THE BOOK OF GENESIS)

Joseph was his father Jacob's favorite son of twelve. When Joseph was approximately seventeen years old he was sold by ten of his jealous brothers into Egyptian slavery while making it appear to his father that he had been killed by an animal.

In Egypt he was taken into the home of the Captain of the Guard. His name was Potiphar. God blessed Joseph there and made Potiphar a prosperous man through Joseph's managerial abilities *(Genesis 39.2)*. Joseph worked hard and honestly and God gave him favor. Potiphar trusted and honored him.

But then along comes the devil's "fly" in the ointment *(Ecclesiastes 10.1)*. Potiphar's wife had seductive and adulterous thoughts toward Joseph. She tried to seduce him on occasions but Joseph would not allow it to happen. During one of her final intensive attempts at seduction Joseph had to run and flee. She was rejected, insulted, and infuriated. "Rape!" she cried.

Joseph lost all his wealth, his character standing in the eyes of others, and was cast into the palace prison. All of this because of a lie and false accusation.

While in prison God gave Joseph favor with the head jailer. He was made a manager over the prison's daily routine and operations. While there he be-friended Pharaoh's butler and asked the butler to remember and help him with his wrongful imprisonment. The butler said he would, but he forgot about Joseph for two full years.

You can tell something of Joseph's character by Potiphar's and the jailer's attitudes of trust toward him. During all of this time he did not manifest one recorded sign of bitterness, hate, or unforgiveness.

He had been betrayed by his own brothers. He had been lied about by a woman whose house had been blessed by Joseph's very presence there. He had been forgotten by a man he had befriended and helped in a desperate time of need. And yet he did not become bitter.

We can be certain that bitterness tried to take of hold of his life as it does anyone in unfair and unjust circumstances. I am certain that the memories of pain, disappointment, disillusionment, hurt, and betrayal sought to destroy him as much as it would any of us. But not once does the Scripture even imply that these things got a foothold in his life (later we will consider why they did not).

You will not find so much as a hint in the Scripture where Joseph said in his heart, "Look at what has happened to me. I can't wait to get out of this jail and settle some scores. I'll find those ten brothers of mine and I'll cut their hearts out. They have dealt me nothing but misery and I hate them! I hate everybody! I hate Potiphar! I hate his wife! I hate that forgetful and ungrateful butler! I hate this country! I hate this jail! I hate life!..."

Remember, the Bible is the one book that never hesitates to reveal the weaknesses of its own heroes of faith. Look carefully and you will find nothing even remotely hinted of concerning this kind of nature being in Joseph.

And then through a sudden and dramatic series of events and revelations, orchestrated by God, Joseph became the highest person of power and authority in Egypt second only to the Pharaoh himself.

Now he was in a position of power to get even with everybody! But no! Joseph got to where he was because he had a believing, forgiving heart. His life was one of constructive design, not destructive disdain.

The day had come, just as God had shown to Joseph back in his teen years *(Genesis 37)*, when his brothers would come and bow down to him (which his brothers did when they later came to Egypt seeking food and subsistence).

When the brothers, who had sold Joseph into slavery, came to the realization of who this was on Egypt's throne, what they had done to him, and the power that was now in Joseph's hand, the situation looked very grave indeed for them.

The story is best told in the words of the scriptures themselves (in fact, if at all possible, you would do well after you have completed this section to go back and read the entire story of Joseph prayerfully and carefully). We will look at an excerpt here:

> 15 When Joseph's brothers saw that their father was dead, they said, "Perhaps Joseph will hate us, and may actually repay us for all the evil which we did to him." 16 So they sent messengers to Joseph, saying, "Before your father died he commanded, saying, 17 'Thus you shall say to Joseph: I beg you, please forgive the trespass of your brothers and their sin; for they did evil to you.'" "Now, please, forgive the trespass of the servants of the God of your father." And Joseph wept when they spoke to him. 18 Then his brothers also went and fell down before his face, and they said, "Behold, we are your servants." *(Genesis 50.15–18 NKJV)*

And what was Joseph's response to all of this? What were his rights? Was this not the opportunity for poetic justice? Did not these brothers deserve any punishment that Joseph might give out?

Listen to the words of Joseph:

> Joseph said to them, "Do not be afraid FOR AM I IN THE PLACE OF GOD?" *(Genesis 50.19 NKJV)*

They had nothing to fear because Joseph had taken care of this long ago apparently through One-Way Forgiveness! Joseph realized that God's hand was in all of this and that it all rose far above his brothers' vicious and destructive envy. He refused to sit in judgment on his offending brothers. This was God's place, and His alone. I doubt seriously that any one reading this book has ever been more grievously treated than Joseph and yet we continue to sit in judgment and harbor an unforgiving spirit! That place of judgment belongs to God and God alone, my friend. You best forgive now! Today!

Joseph continued:

[20] "But as for you, you meant evil against me; but God meant it for good, in order to bring it about as it is this day, to save many people alive. [21] Now therefore, do not be afraid; I will provide for you and your little ones." And he comforted them and spoke kindly to them. *(Genesis 50.20–21 NKJV)*

Take just a serious moment or two and let this entire account sink deeply into your heart and thinking.

Just think of what would have happened if Joseph had been a vindictive person.

What if Joseph had destroyed these people? What would have become of the nation Israel? What would have happened to the Scriptures that have come to us through them? What about Judah, one of the twelve of Israel, through whom the physical lineage and seed of Christ came?

These and many other questions like them show the serious consequences of forgiveness and unforgiveness!

Joseph's great-grandfather Abraham had made his contribution in faith. So had his grandfather Isaac. And his father Jacob. But the work of God is never dependent upon one person alone, but upon every member of the people of God in the coming generations functioning in their place, whether great or small.

Joseph's forgiveness loosed the work of God to continue in and through Israel in a very definite sense. His unforgiveness could have severely bound and limited the work of God for several generations of time.

Joseph *"comforted"* them. He spoke *"kindly"* to them. He FORGAVE them. Consider again Colossians 3.12–14 and Ephesians 4.30–32 printed in the opening *(and conclusion)* of this Section 4 in the light of Joseph's response toward his maliciously offending brothers.

Let God inspire your heart again to new heights of faith in Him as you read for yourself this marvelous account of God's wisdom and grace at work in Joseph's life in Genesis, chapters 37—50.

God give and grant us people with the heart of Joseph in His Kingdom today. How desperately this kind of heart is needed in churches, marriages and homes now!

What if Joseph had become bitter toward God for allowing all of these things to happen to him? What if he had allowed bitterness to sour him and destroy his relationship with the Lord and his God-given prophetic destiny?

Where there are offenses, whether real or imagined, there will be injury and hurt that will require forgiveness in order for there to be a healing.

The people of Nazareth were offended at Jesus and their bitterness produced unbelief that bound the Lord so that He could do no mighty miracles there in their lives or community.

Mark writing of this turning point occasion for both Jesus and Nazareth said:

> [3] ...And they were offended at Him ... [5] Now He could do no might works there, except that He laid His hands a few sick people and healed them. [6] And He marveled because of their unbelief ... *(Mark 6.3-6 NKJV).*

The people of Nazareth's being offended by Jesus and consequently not believing in Him necessitated His having to leave His home town of Nazareth and relocate in Capernaum.

The people of Jesus' generation being offended by Jesus' teachings, claims, and miracles took our Lord Jesus

> "who went about doing good, and healing all who were oppressed of the devil" *(Acts 10.38 NKJV)*

and treated Him like a common criminal. He received one of the cruelest mockeries of justice in the history of the world. He was brutally beaten and shamefully treated. He was lied against. People tried to twist the meaning of His words out of context. He was mocked. And, finally, He was painfully, disgracefully, and unjustly crucified.

Jesus uttered seven words (statements or utterances) from the cruel and unjust Cross of His agonizing death.

What was the FIRST word? Listen.

> "Father, FORGIVE them; for they do not know what they do" *(Luke 23.34 NKJV)*

Is there a record of anyone standing around Jesus' cross that day asking for forgiveness? No, not one person is said to have asked for forgiveness! They were mocking. Gambling. Ridiculing. A few were weeping. But, there was no one recorded as asking for forgiveness when Jesus spoke these words on the cross (the repentant thief would reach out to Him a little later to be remembered by Jesus)!

But, Jesus as the Son of man forgave them. With One-Way forgiveness. He opened the door in His heart of grace to them so that they, when they repented and turned to Him, would find a Throne of mercy and grace *(Hebrews 4.16)*.

In Acts, chapter 2, Peter preached to many of the very ones that had crucified Jesus fifty to fifty-three days previously, saying,

"...God has made this Jesus, whom YOU crucified, both Lord and Christ" *(Acts 2.36 NKJV. See the entire chapter)*

What did God offer them on that day in Acts 2?

"REMISSION of sins" *(Acts 2.38)!*

That is, FORGIVENESS!

How did it happen? Jesus LOOSED the situation for them some fifty or so days previous to this when He said, *"Father, FORGIVE them"*. This opened the door for the Holy Spirit to work in conviction and bring them to a place of repentance so that they could receive the ultimate work of God—the forgiveness and remission of their sins.

Because Jesus loosed the situation through one dynamic aspect of forgiveness from the cross it made possible the ultimate dynamic aspect of forgiveness in being forgiven, cleansed, and delivered from sin. Jesus removed the hindrance to the mighty work of the Holy Spirit's in convicting men of their sins—both known and unknown sins. Three thousand were saved that day! And that was just the beginning.

We need to stop NOW grieving the heart of the Holy Spirit. Let us NOW get about the business of forgiving.

In obedient faith begin NOW to loose your home! Loose your marriage! Loose your church! Loose your friends! Loose your pastor! Loose your congregation! Loose the Holy Spirit! Loose YOURSELF!

[30] And DO NOT GRIEVE THE HOLY SPIRIT of God, by whom you were sealed for the day of redemption.
[31] Let ALL bitterness, wrath, anger, clamor, and evil speaking be put away from you, with ALL malice.

[32] AND be kind to one another, tenderhearted, FORGIVING one another, JUST AS God in Christ FORGAVE YOU. *(Ephesians 4.30–32 NKJV)*

[12] Therefore, as the elect of God, holy and beloved, put on tender mercies, kindness, humility, meekness, longsuffering;
[13] BEARING WITH one another, and FORGIVING one another, if anyone has a complaint against another; EVEN AS Christ forgave you, SO YOU ALSO MUST DO. *(Colossians 3.12-13 NKJV)*

# WE ARE NOT WAITING ON GOD – GOD IS WAITING ON US!

# THOUGHTS

"Behold, I stand at the door and knock. If anyone hears My voice and opens the door, I will come in to him and dine with him, and he with Me" *(Revelation 3:20 NKJV)*.

**ONE-WAY FORGIVENESS**. Through One-Way Forgiveness we release in our heart the debts of offensive hurt we feel is owed to us by an offender, or offenders, or even offending circumstances.

Forgiveness is letting go and releasing the aughts we have against the anys of our life. It does not in any way justify or cleanse an offender for or from the wrong or the sin they may have committed against us and ultimately against God. Nor does it automatically produce reconciliation between us and the person(s) that we experienced the offense with.

However, one-way forgiveness does release us from the bitter fall-out of ill-will we may harbor in our heart toward others and it does open the door of our offended heart to reconciliation which means that there is only one door closed now instead of two or more.

The opened door of our heart has responded to the knocking and voice of Jesus to His invitation to restore us to the fullness and freshness of fellowship with Him.

One-Way forgiveness opens the door of our heart to Jesus' voice and knocking so the situation of offense has only one or so other doors remaining closed at which Jesus will faithfully knock and call.

If and when those remaining closed doors are opened to our Lord's knocking and invitation then that person will find our door that was closed already opened and we are ready for reconciliation through forgiveness that we have already put into place.

One-Way forgiveness keeps us reconciled to the Lord and His Presence and fellowship in our lives. This is the primary reconciliation that is absolutely essential to our walk in our Lord's fullness of power.

**FORGIVENESS AND OFFENSES**. There are various levels of offenses that we experience in life and there are corresponding dynamics of forgiveness to effectively resolve them.

There are offenses that involve a deep darkness of sin such as we would experience in a violent kidnapping, a home break in involving great trauma and pain for our person and/or family, sadistic torture, sexual abuse, cruel and merciless murder, and like offenses.

Then there are yet other deep life altering offenses that happen such as with a drunk driver (or a driver on drugs) that in a senseless accident takes away members of our family or may leave us permanently disabled for life—or both! There are increasingly similar outcomes that may happen when someone is texting while driving or in other ways allow themselves to become distracted and careless resulting in similar life altering tragedies.

There are the deep offenses involving adultery and betrayal when one's spouse is unfaithful to the other and enters into a sexual or similar affair with someone outside of their marriage bond. Or become involved in pornography and other perverted lifestyles that defile the holy marriage union.

There are divorces involving the loss of children, possessions, finances, love, and security. It has been shown that the loss of our spouse through divorce can be far more cruel and devastating than natural or accidental death. Divorce involves a separation by rejection and choice plus the shattering of one's family and children.

There are the loss of jobs and positions with the security that comes with a steady income. Or being passed over for a deserved promotion due to an adversarial overseer, or nepotism toward someone else less qualified. Or those who hurt your business with unfair tactics or deliberate intent.

There are offenses that involve fraud, robbing, stealing, ID theft, being cheated out of one's wages of labor, and more.

The above offenses are life altering and each involve different levels of approach in forgiveness and resolve. There may not always be reconciliation in such cases except within the heart of the person who releases and commits it to the Lord.

Then there are offenses caused by thoughtless acts that cause deep hurt within us that involve injustices (real or imagined), lying, malicious gossip, slander, betrayal of friendships, thoughtless actions and harsh words such as occur in marriages, homes, families, churches, and the like.

And there are offenses that occur within us because we misunderstand, or we see or think something that is not the actual reality of the situation, or what is really happening. We imagine a twisted version of it.

Somewhat surprisingly the closer you get to the bottom of the offense list is where the vast majority of wide spread damage and division in people's lives, marriages, homes, and churches today occur. Most of us have not been involved in a kidnapping, home break in, sadistic torture, and like offenses.

For the vast majority of us the troubling offenses we battle begin with at the bottom of this offense list and diminish in number (though increasing in intensity) as you work up toward the top.

Still, in all of the fore mentioned offenses and the others that would fit into one of those or a similar category we must find a way to forgive in the sense of releasing our hearts and minds from the binding forces of any type of offense and loosening ourselves to the deep workings of God's grace, Holy Spirit, and Word.

We must allow God's grace and plans for our lives to define our life and not offenses. We must allow the God Who somehow, someway makes all things work together for our good when it is all said and done.

"And we know that ALL things work together for good to those who love God, to those who are the called according to His purpose." *(Romans 8.28 NKJV)*

God will give you direction in all of these areas. You put into place and allow the principles and dynamics of forgiveness to work in your life and situation. God will be faithful to give us direction.

It is forgiveness in the sense of releasing ourselves from the destructive offenses of others to embrace the constructive that will determine if we live blessed rather than cursed; to walk in light rather than in gloom and darkness; to live in joy and hope rather than perpetual pain and despair.

The one, critical, basic of forgiveness that must transpire in our lives is that which is between our self and God. There must be that dynamic of forgiveness that leads us to complete reconciliation and agreement with the heart of God for all and any offenses coming from others along with their hurts that have happened in our life.

It is then that God can work in and through us to facilitate any and all possible reconciliations that may exist between our self and other persons or situations in life while bringing down any strongholds of darkness that may be planted in our heart.

But it must first happen in us. The closed door of our heart must first be opened to the Lordship of Christ and to any reconciliation that God can occasion between our self and any others.

The AUGHT in our heart toward all our ANYS must first be resolved through God's work of grace and love bringing forth in us true forgiveness and release from all bitterness, anger, malice, hurt, ill-will, and the like.

**LIFE IS ABOUT CHOICES**. And choices are about consequences. Every choice we make in our life have ripple, rapture, or rupture effects that shape what our life is going to be—for better or for worse. For time and for eternity. For the people of a person's present time and the posterity that will follow afterwards.

NO CHOICE IS A CHOICE. I am sure that most if not all of us have heard this truism. Mistakenly we think that only choices that involve action are the kind of choices that affect our life. But in truth every inactive response we take still involves a choice. When God is dealing with our lives and we say, "I will wait until another time"—that is still a choice. Until "another time" we have made a choice of saying "no" for the present time—and there may not be "another time" when that choice can validly or effectively be reversed to a "yes".

"For He says: '*In an acceptable time I have heard you, And in the day of salvation I have helped you.*' Behold, **now** *is* the accepted time; behold, **now** *is* the day of salvation" (*II Corinthians 6.2* NKJV—**now** *is made* **bold** *here for emphasis*).

Do not wait to pray, forgive, and loose the full work of the Lord in your life and in other lives. Do it NOW. Tomorrow may be too late.

# QUESTIONS

1. What are the different kinds, aspects, and dynamics of love that we talked about in this section? What does it illustrate for us when considering what forgiveness is and is not?

2. What are some of the different aspects and dynamics of forgiveness that was discussed in this section?

3. What is meant by the thoughts of Two-Way Forgiveness and One-Way Forgiveness?

4. What is wrong with the old saying: "Forgive and forget"?

5. What happens to the memories and feelings of hurt and resentment when we forgive?

6. What is meant by the statement that forgiveness is not a religious ritual but the forging of right relationships?

7. How does the life of Joseph demonstrate for us what forgiveness is and does?

8. What does Jesus' home town of Nazareth show to us about the deadliness of being and remaining offended?

9. What does Jesus' first word from the cross of *"Father, forgive them, for they do not know what they do"* show us about forgiveness?

10. In Thoughts how do you understand the author's point on One-Way forgiveness in the light of your relationship to God?

# SECTION FIVE

---

# WHY OUR FORGIVENESS MUST BE UNCONDITIONAL

---

# LUKE 6.27–28, 31–38 *(NKJV)*

<sup>27</sup> But I say to you who hear: Love your enemies, do good to those who hate you,

<sup>28</sup> bless those who curse you, and pray for those who spitefully use you.

<sup>31</sup> And just as you want men to do to you, you also do to them likewise.

<sup>32</sup> But if you love those who love you, what credit is that to you? For even sinners love those who love them.

<sup>33</sup> And if you do good to those who do good to you, what credit is that to you? For even sinners do the same.

<sup>34</sup> And if you lend *to those* from whom you hope to receive back, what credit is that to you? For even sinners lend to sinners to receive as much back.

<sup>35</sup> But love your enemies, do good, and lend, hoping for nothing in return; and your reward will be great, and you will be sons of the Most High. For He is kind to the unthankful and evil.

<sup>36</sup> Therefore be merciful, just as your Father also is merciful.

<sup>37</sup> Judge not, and you shall not be judged. Condemn not, and you shall not be condemned. **Forgive, and you will be forgiven.**

<sup>38</sup> Give, and it will be given to you: good measure, pressed down, shaken together, and running over will be put into your bosom. For with the same measure that you use, it will be measured back to you.

# OUR JOURNEY TOGETHER THUS FAR

Up to this point we have considered together what I feel the Holy Spirit through numerous Scriptures has impressed to my heart concerning the impossibility of not being offended from time to time in our lives and our offending others.

We then considered how to deal with the offenses by the ultimate dynamics of forgiveness plus other truths that help us to understand the broader picture in which forgiveness is set.

We have sought to show the binding power of unforgiveness and the loosening power of forgiveness.

I have stressed, as I believe the Holy Spirit has to my heart, that forgiveness is essential not just for our church life but for our homes, families, marriages, personal interrelationships, and the challenges of living out our lives. To seeing certain prayers fully answered. To seeing the promises of God fully come to pass versus just partial if any in fulfillment.

I have emphasized, from the scriptures, how forgiveness is essential because human life is essential in the eyes of our Creator-Father-God. That we must seek to see the full picture rather than just pieces and parts. That we must make a choice of whether we are going to be builders of lives or destroyers of lives, encouragers or discouragers, a bridge or a wall.

Then I pointed out to you some of the things that have been mistaken for forgiveness and, in contrast, what forgiveness really is.

Now we come to one more important dynamic of forgiveness that came to my heart on that Saturday and the days following about these dynamics of forgiveness. In this section we will consider two other basic dynamics concerning forgiveness before going considering **How to Forgive**.

I believe that it is important at this point to understand these two other basic principles concerning forgiveness in order to better understand what aspect of forgiveness we are writing about that truly helps bring about the restoring and health of our relationships with God and others.

## WHY GOD'S FORGIVENESS IS CONDITIONAL

In the last chapter of the Old Testament book of Joshua, chapter 24, Joshua gives a challenge to Israel who had finally entered and began possessing the Promised Land as he says:

"...choose for yourselves this day whom you will serve...But as for me and my house we will serve the LORD" *(Joshua 24.15 NKJV).*

To this challenge of serving God the Israelites in what must have been, I believe, shallow emotions replied:

"We also will serve the LORD, for He is our God" *(Joshua 24.18 NKJV).*

Joshua, who had spent so many years in the presence of God and living with a very obstinate people during his training under Moses, knew that the Israelites had replied from a shallow state of emotions rather than a thought out understanding based on the realities of God's Person versus just His power. Knowing their history and tendencies he said,

"You cannot serve the LORD, for He is a holy God. He is a jealous God; He will not forgive your transgressions nor your sins" *(Joshua 24.19 NKJV).*

What exactly was happening here? In one instance Joshua was telling the people they must serve God and challenging them to do the same. In the next instance it appears that Joshua was telling the people that they could not do what they must!

Joshua had stated that he and his house would serve the Lord. His decision was based on many years of coming to know the Lord's heart and mind for their times along with his life and relationship to the Lord. His was many years of commitment based on the knowledge of God's expectations.

Joshua, I believe, was telling the people that God's very Person and essence was holy. Serving God in an emotional response because of His power alone would never be enough. They still did not grasp and truly understand the holy nature of God and therefore would not follow His instructions on how to be rightly related to Him.

Since He is a holy God this means that He will not be served by an unholy people *(Exodus 19.6; Leviticus 11.44, 19.2, 20.26; I Peter 1.15–16).* If the people did not grasp this and trust in God's Word to them they would not find the needed forgiveness.

Actually, I believe an important point is being made here that is repeated in numerous ways throughout the Scriptures.

Joshua knew that the people were not understanding a critical truth. Before they could serve God the SIN QUESTION must be properly dealt with. God's very nature of holiness and purity demanded that every question and taint of sin be dealt with and resolved before there could be genuine ongoing fellowship with Him.

Joshua's statement was a part of the continuing, step-by-step revelation in the Scriptures of the nature of God and man's nature. God's nature is holy. Man's nature is sinful.

This continuing step-by-step revelation would bring to all of us the reality and provision of the fullness of God's salvation in the Person of Jesus Christ and His sacrifice on the cross, resurrection from the dead, ascension back to heaven, and the outpouring of the HOLY Spirit as recorded in Acts 2 f. and Romans, chapters 3 through 5—and numerous other key Scriptures.

The ultimate work of Christ to deal with sin was foreshadowed in all of the sacrifices, feast days, and other like directives that God gave to Israel in the Old Testament to be done in faith until the debt of sin was paid in full by Christ.

Just as it is with extreme heat and cold there is absolutely no fellowship between holiness and sin. When extreme heat and cold come together there is explosive violence resulting in devastating storms and destruction.

Take a glass or a cup that has been in a freezer and pour boiling water into it and the glass or cup will literally blow apart. There can be no lasting relationship between the two. The one cannot contain the other. So it is with sin and holiness. One cannot exist where the other is.

Man's sin must be resolved before there can be fellowship with a holy God. The only way that this resolve can come is through FORGIVENESS. The only way forgiveness can come is through CONFESSION of sin, REPENTANCE from sin, and OBEDIENT FAITH in God's salvation through the vicarious work of our Lord Jesus Christ.

Israel was not really applying the revelation that God had given them concerning His holiness to this point in time when Joshua challenged the people. Consequently Joshua understood God could not forgive them until they responded to Him in obedient faith—not just empty words of emotion. God could not forgive them until there was true faith, confession and repentance from sin, coupled with an obedient faith to follow Him.

**This brings out a very important point**. Because ONLY God is the ultimate of holiness, ONLY He can comprehend the depths and workings of sin and consequently demand the CONDITIONS required to correct the situation.

What I am saying is that ONLY God is in the place to JUDGE so only He can demand a CONDITIONAL FORGIVENESS.

In the Book of Revelation, the very last book of the Bible, as God's judgments are being poured out on unrepentant mankind the following statement is made concerning His righteous character to call mankind into account:

> **ONLY God is in the place to JUDGE so only He can demand a CONDITIONAL FORGIVENESS.**

⁴ Then the third angel poured out his bowl on the rivers and springs of water, and they became blood.
⁵ And I heard the angel of the waters saying: "You are righteous, O Lord, The One who is and who was and who to be, Because You have judged these things.
⁶ For they have shed the blood of saints and prophets, And You have given them blood to drink. For it is their just due."
⁷ And I heard another from the altar saying, "Even so, Lord God Almighty, true and righteous *are* Your judgments." *(Revelation 16.4-7 NKJV)*

In our previous section we considered the fear that Joseph's brothers had when Jacob their father died. They feared that after their father's death Joseph would seek revenge and retribution for what they had maliciously and intentionally done to him. In trembling and fear they knelt before him pleading for mercy and forgiveness.

Joseph, you remember, at this time occupied one of the highest positions in the most powerful government of the world at that point in history. He had power. He had wisdom. He was knowledgeable. He was honored. He could get revenge and no human being would have thought badly toward him for doing so. He had both might and right on his side.

And yet, he refused to hold his brothers in judgment for their horrible and intentional offense! Why? Again, in his own words:

"Do not be afraid, for am I IN THE PLACE OF GOD?" *(Genesis 50.19 NKJV)*

One of the things that marked Joseph as a great man of God was the fact he knew his place of limitations and he knew God's place of supremacy. Joseph, nor any other man without divine revelation, could judge the human heart. Only God can do this. Judgment must be reserved for the only One capable of justly administering it.

Only God knows the real motivations, intentions, and purposes of our hearts. We see outward actions. We seek to interpret them, but overwhelmingly for the most part our judgments are incomplete and fallible because, as I have stated previously, our knowledge is partial and we see through a glass darkly as it were. *(see I Corinthians 13.8–13)*

God, too, sees the outward actions, but before the deed was ever done God had also seen exactly what was in us that caused that deed!

Therefore, VENGEANCE BELONGS TO GOD, and to God alone!

*"Beloved, do not avenge yourselves, but rather GIVE PLACE to wrath; for it is written, 'Vengeance is MINE, I will repay,' says the Lord." (Romans 12.19 NKJV—also see Deuteronomy 32.35, Psalm 94.1, Hebrews 10.30)*

When we seek to take revenge on someone, whether it is by an outward act or an inward grudge such as withdrawing our love, saying hurtful things, or turning on the offender, we are taking that which belongs to God alone! We are in danger of becoming guilty of a greater offense than the one that has offended us.

The *"condemnation"* of *"the devil"* was when he uttered the words *"I will"* and in the sin of pride dared to try and take the place that belongs only to God Himself! *(I Timothy 3.6 cf. Isaiah 14.12–15)*

When we forGIVE we GIVE PLACE to God's position and authority. We leave that which belongs to Him to use as He alone knows how and when to use!

> When we forGIVE we GIVE PLACE to God's position and authority.

For these and other reasons, only God can make forgiveness a conditional thing.

*NOTE: If there is a question in your mind about what we are discussing here and how Scriptural discipline fits into conditional and unconditional forgiveness please see my comments in the Thoughts article at the close of this section.*

## WHY OUR FORGIVENESS MUST BE UNCONDITIONAL

Now, as we did with what forgiveness is and is not, we will again contrast and reverse some of the things that we considered about why only God's forgiveness can be conditional.

God is holy. But concerning our person and lives the scriptures uniformly declare:

"for ALL have sinned, and fall short of the glory of God" *(Romans 3.23 NKJV)*

"...There is NONE righteous, no, not one" *(Romans 3.10 NKJV)*

"ALL we like sheep have gone astray; we have turned, EVERY ONE, to his own way..." *(Isaiah 53.6 NKJV).*

Therefore, our forgiveness must be unconditional because of our fleshly or carnal sin-nature.

How vividly this is illustrated in the ministry of our Lord Jesus concerning a woman who had been caught in the very act of adultery *(John 8.1–11)*. There was no denying the evidence. She had sinned. Witnesses had seen it. It was verified. She was guilty (and so was the man that they never bothered to bring).

They brought her to Jesus. They began to clamor. The Law demanded she be stoned to death (along with the man that they did not bring). They ask how He would judge her.

He stooped down to write in the dirt. Silence. They continued to badger Jesus to pass judgment on her. Finally He replied,

"...He that is without sin among you, let him first cast a stone at her" *(John 8.7 NKJV)*

Jesus again stooped down and continued to write on the ground. Silence.

One by one, quietly and sheepishly, the accusing men in the crowd slipped away. Suddenly their judgment had turned in upon themselves and it was devastating. How it hit home. What an impact personal revelation from God concerning our own life brings to our awareness!

There had been no thought or consideration of forgiveness in the hearts of that crowd of men. Their only thought was judgment and punishment. Healing was the furthest thing from their minds. Eradication not edification was their objective. They did not even really care what happened to the woman, right or wrong. The fact is, their ultimate and real goal was to use this to entrap Jesus.

*"He that is without sin"!* How this revealed the inability of men to be in the place that belongs only to God in passing judgment. How can we set stipulations on our personal forgiveness of others? Only God's forgiveness can be conditional.

## OUR FORGIVENESS MUST BE UNCONDITIONAL BECAUSE OF WHAT WE ARE REALLY UP AGAINST

"For we are not wrestling with flesh and blood [contending only with physical opponents], but against the despotisms, against the powers, against [the master spirits who are] the world rulers of this present darkness, against the spirit forces of wickedness in the heavenly (supernatural) sphere" *(Ephesians 6.12 Amplified Bible).*

For you and I to pass judgment on others and insist upon a conditional forgiveness *(our conditions, of course)* is to play into the hands of Satan, the archenemy of our souls, as well as caving in to our own sinful tendencies. It is to give Satan a foothold in our lives that opens our lives to dark forces and mind-sets that will sooner or later wreak destruction in our life, home, family, marriage, and/or church.

It is very important we truly grasp this in our hearts. We must be vigilant and fortify our hearts against any and all footholds of the satanic and demonic that will eventually become strongholds in our own life—especially as we rapidly escalate toward the prophetic end-times.

Our battle is with very real and formidable forces of darkness that are satanic and demonic. More times than we may realize these *"power(s) of darkness"* *(Colossians 1.13 cf. Ephesians 6.12)* manifest themselves through the sinful flesh-nature of the human heart. This includes the heart of our loved ones and our friends along with others that may offend us.

It is extremely difficult, indeed, many times impossible in our limited and partial understanding alone, to know where the one begins and the other ends.

It is very foolish and futile for us to fight the bow that was used to empower *"the arrow that flies by day"* *(Psalms 91.5 NKJV)* rather than the one who employed the bow for destructive purposes!

When the Lord asked His disciples who they thought He, Jesus, truly is, it was Peter who stated, *"You are the Christ, the Son of the living God."* And then just a short time later when Jesus, the Son of the living God, was telling Peter and the others about His approaching crucifixion it was Peter who was disputing Jesus' very words with the statement,

"this shall not happen to you" *(Matthew 16.16, 22 NKJV).*

How did our Lord Jesus respond? He said, *"you are an offense to me."* But NOT to Peter whose voice had wrongly rebuked Him. As you read that entire verse you find that it was Satan Jesus was speaking to when He said,

"Get behind me, SATAN: YOU are an offense to Me, for you are not mindful of the things of God, but the things of men" *(Matthew 16.23 NKJV)*.

Jesus readily recognized that it was Peter's mind that contained the thought and his mouth that uttered the words of that thought. But His full rebuke revealed that it was Satan who had planted both there!

Jesus did not rebuke the bow. He reached up and deflected the arrow fired from the bow. There was consequently no wound. Thus He bound Satan's offense against Him—not Peter. He addressed the very one that had used Peter.

Peter was the instrument, or bow, so to speak. But Satan was the culprit who had loaded the bow with the arrow of lying offense and fired it through the lips of Peter.

Think back with me once again to Joseph and his forgiving heart toward his brothers. How could he have compassion on those who had sought to destroy his very life, who had robbed him of his home, family, friends, place of belonging, and homeland for so many years?

Joseph realized something that many Christians have tragically failed to realize. His brother's anger was ultimately directed at the dreams of revelation God had given to him *(Genesis 37.5–11)*. They determined to destroy and rid themselves of *"this dreamer"* or *"master of dreams"* *(Genesis 37.19)*.

This very revelation from God that caused his brothers to want to kill him was the very thing that kept Joseph, I believe, filled with a forgiving heart rather than a bitter spirit.

In Joseph's own words,

"...you meant evil against me but GOD MEANT IT for good..." *(Genesis 50.20 NKJV)*

Although the satanic element and spiritual conflict is not directly referred to, Joseph looked beyond the flesh and blood element involved in the situation to God Who had foreseen and foretold of what He was going to do through Joseph. All of this was before the first of the thirty-nine books of the Old Testament was even completed (with the possible exception of Job), much less the New Testament.

Until we listen with an obedient believing heart to the word of God, we will not be able to comprehend the basic dynamics involved in the forgiveness process.

## Our Forgiveness Must Be Unconditional Because of What God Says to Us in His Word

[4] Who are you to judge another's servant? To his own master he stands or falls. Indeed, he will be made to stand, for God is able to make him stand. [10] But why do you judge your brother? Or why do you show contempt for your brother? For we shall all stand before the judgment seat of Christ. [12] So then each of us shall give account of himself to God. [13] Therefore let us not judge one another anymore, but rather resolve this, not to put a stumbling block or a cause to fall in our brother's way. *(Romans 14.4, 10, 12–13 NKJV)*

Jesus Himself taught us very specifically that we are not to be judgmental when He said,

[1] "Judge not, that you be not judged. [2] For with what judgment you judge, you will be judged; and with the measure you use, it will be measured back to you. [3] And why do you look at the speck in your brother's eye, but do not consider the plank in your own eye?" *(Matthew 7.1-3 NKJV)*

Many of us have read and heard these words of our Lord so often that we have allowed their effectiveness for us as the very revelation of the Father's heart and will slip from being actively applied in our lives. But that does not change the absoluteness of their truth nor the seriousness with which our Lord gave them to us!

That same Spirit of Christ was still speaking when Paul wrote to all Christians,

"Therefore judge nothing before the time, until the Lord comes, who will both bring to light the hidden things of darkness and reveal the counsels of the hearts. Then each one's praise will come from God" *(I Corinthians 4.5 NKJV)*.

## Our Forgiveness Must Be Unconditional Because Our Basic Kingdom Relationships with Each Other Demand That We Forgive *(Matthew 18.21–35)*

How clear the words of our Lord Jesus are in regards to our maintaining what is right in the sight of the Lord in our relationships with one another.

[23] "Therefore if you bring your gift to the altar, and there remember that your brother has something against you, [24] leave your gift there before the altar, and go your way. First be reconciled to your brother, and then come and offer your gift" *(Matthew 5.23–24 NKJV).*

## OUR FORGIVENESS MUST BE UNCONDITIONAL BECAUSE SUCH IS ESSENTIAL TO OUR CHRISTIAN WALK OF FREEDOM AND LIBERTY

It is impossible for the work of our Lord Jesus Christ to continue to fully flow in and through us unless we have a heart of forgiveness.

I believe it is important at this point to remember the forgiveness we are talking of here is dealing with issues in our own hearts and minds that create bitterness, hurt, feelings of ill-will, condemnation of others, and the like that poisons us and becomes a sinful attitude and mind-set that results in divisions, strife, hate, fighting, and the like.

We are speaking of the dynamic and aspect of forgiveness in which we release others from the debt we feel they owe us so that we can walk in freedom and fullness of Spirit-filled living.

How could the words of Jesus possibly have any fulfillment for us and others if forgiveness does not accompany them.

"The Spirit of the LORD is upon Me, because HE HAS ANOINTED Me TO preach the gospel to the poor; He has sent Me TO heal the brokenhearted, TO proclaim liberty to the captives and recovery of sight to the blind, TO set at liberty those who are oppressed; TO proclaim the acceptable year of the LORD" *(Luke 4.18–19 NKJV)*

It does not take any great thinking to see that the spirit of UNforgiveness will work directly to UNdo everything that God has anointed us "TO" do. Only in the spirit of forgiveness can we get beyond the many varied offenses that are impossible to avoid in life and have the anointing of the Holy Spirit bring these ministries and purposes to pass through our lives!

## OUR FORGIVENESS MUST BE UNCONDITIONAL BECAUSE WE NEED SUCH FORGIVENESS OURSELVES

Read again, very prayerfully, Luke 6.27–28, 31–38 that we placed at the beginning of this section. We are to do to others as we need to have done to us! There is no mistaking what Jesus is saying there.

When we give mercy, compassion, forgiveness, and the like (not just money) it is going to be returned to us pressed down, shaken together, and running over with good measure!

God's forgiveness is CONDITIONAL because God IS God. Our forgiveness must be UN-CONDITIONAL because we are NOT God.

When you begin to understand in your heart these basic truths and dynamics of forgiveness *(of which we have only mentioned a few in this section)* then you will begin to realize our position and relationship to the type of forgiveness that works to restore our hearts to a right relationship with God and others.

Now we are ready to consider the proverbial "where-the-rubber-meets-the-road" truth on **HOW TO FORGIVE**.

> God's forgiveness is CONDITIONAL because God IS God. Our forgiveness must be UN-CONDITIONAL because we are NOT God.

121

# THOUGHTS

WE MUST NOT CONFUSE GOD ORDAINED DISCIPLINE SUCH AS THAT DESCRIBED IN Matthew 18.17, Romans 16.17, I Corinthians 5.9f, and like Scriptures with our consideration of CONDITIONAL and UNCONDITIONAL FORGIVENESS.

We can exercise a judgment of discipline. In fact, there are times when we MUST act in a judgment of discipline. This is especially true when it has to do with positions of leadership and influence in the church.

But always we must maintain a heart and mindset of restoring a person in their walk with the Lord and forgiveness in our relationship to them. You can correct and discipline, within scriptural guidelines, with a heart of forgiveness and a hope of restoring while at the same time protecting people as much as possible from a destructive influence and maintaining a Christ honoring testimony.

What I am saying about forgiveness is not to imply or encourage passiveness toward sin or destructive elements of human nature. There is discipline that must be administered at times that requires a certain type of judging.

But always this type of discipline is to be within Scriptural boundaries and directives. It is a judgment by government and leadership ordained of God Himself whether in the church, the political realm, the home, etc.

Discipline when Scriptural, YES. Bitterness, harshness, unkindness, revenge, hate, and the like toward the offender, NO AND NEVER! You can be firm in discipline and still be compassionate, loving, and forgiving.

There are some things that we are Scripturally directed to deal with. There are other things that we simply cannot deal with (such as Jesus talks of in the parable of the TARES AND WHEAT in Matthew 13.24–30, 36–43) and must be left in hands of God and His appointed holy angels until the day and time of judgments that God has appointed and ordained in His Own wisdom.

Even when a person does not accept the discipline required for restoration, or the offense is such that we cannot restore the erring one to their former status or position, we still need to have a forgiving heart toward that individual.

This does not mean we condone the wrong, but that we honor God's position to pass final judgment and sentence. We release the person(s) and situation to God while we do what He has instructed us to do for the sake of His kingdom and church.

Something else has impressed my heart since becoming so aware of the necessity of unconditional forgiveness and the seriousness of our judging everybody and everything in people's lives.

There appears to be a very distinct difference between the general ministry of most of us in ministry today and that of the apostle and prophet. One of the elements in the ministry of the apostle and prophet is the fact that God *has* committed, it appears to me, a certain amount of judgment to them in keeping with their office that others are not enabled by Him of pronouncing and doing.

And it would appear that there are rare instances when God in His Sovereign wisdom may speak and/work a judgment through a person on special occasions of need.

There seems to be an anointing and revelation for the occasion on which to pass that particular element of judgment *(e.g., Acts 5.1–11)*. This appears to be exceptional and not general. At this writing I have not researched this area as thoroughly as I would like, but what little from time to time I have been able to do continues to strengthen this conviction in me.

# QUESTIONS

1. Why does God's forgiveness contain conditions?

2. What is the sin problem that must be taken into account when thinking about God's forgiveness being conditional?

3. What are some of the reasons our forgiveness has to be unconditional as set forth in this section?

4. What are some of the dangers of making our forgiveness conditional? *(Remember, we are not talking about appropriate church type discipline that may be needed to protect the church's position in its community and that is designed to give opportunity for the restoration of a Christian who has fallen into deep sin nor of discipline needed in certain home situations, etc)*

5. In Thoughts what is the author saying about the differences between God Ordained Discipline and the Dynamics of Forgiveness?

# SECTION SIX

---

# HOW TO FORGIVE

---

## THE FIVE STEPS TO FORGIVENESS

# MATTHEW 6.9-15 *(NKJV)*

⁹ In this manner, therefore, pray: Our Father in heaven, Hallowed be Your name.

¹⁰ Your kingdom come. Your will be done on earth as *it is* in heaven.

¹¹ Give us this day our daily bread.

¹² And forgive us our debts, as we forgive our debtors.

¹³ And do not lead us into temptation, but deliver us from the evil one. For Yours is the kingdom and the power and the glory forever. Amen.

¹⁴ For if you forgive men their trespasses, your heavenly Father will also forgive you.

¹⁵ But if you do not forgive men their trespasses, neither will your Father forgive your trespasses.

# MARK 11.22-26 *(NKJV)*

²² So Jesus answered and said to them, "Have faith in God.

²³ "For assuredly, I say to you, whoever SAYS to this mountain, 'Be removed and be cast into the sea,' and does NOT DOUBT in his heart, but BELIEVES that those things he SAYS will be done, he will have whatever he SAYS.

²⁴ "Therefore I say to you, whatever things you ASK when you PRAY, BELIEVE that you receive *them*, and you will have *them*.

²⁵ "AND whenever you stand PRAYING, if you have anything against anyone, FORGIVE him, that your Father in heaven may also forgive you your trespasses.

²⁶ "But if you do not forgive, neither will your Father in heaven forgive your trespasses."

# MATTHEW 18.35 *(NKJV)*

So My heavenly Father also will do to you if each of you, from his heart, does not forgive his brother his trespasses.

# JAMES 2.13 *(NKJV)*

For judgment is without mercy to the one who has shown no mercy. Mercy triumphs over judgment.

**JAMES 2.13** *(The Living Bible)* For there will be no mercy to those who have shown no mercy. But if you have been merciful, then God's mercy toward you will win out over his judgment against you.

**JAMES 2.13** *(New Living Translation)* There will be no mercy for those who have not shown mercy to others. But if you have been merciful, God will be merciful when he judges you.

## EPHESIANS 4.32 *(NKJV)*

And be kind to one another, tenderhearted, forgiving one another, just as God in Christ forgave you.

# Five Steps to Forgiveness

I trust at this point that you have some new insights into forgiveness and would agree that we need to forgive. And I trust that you are seeing that the dynamics of forgiveness can accomplish much more than you have previously realized in stopping the crushing hurts of offenses that may be stopping you.

The vital question to us at this point is: HOW CAN I FORGIVE? Or, HOW DO I FORGIVE?

The following five steps in the dynamics of forgiveness, I believe, will help carry you across the forgiveness threshold into new peace, joy, and power in the Lord. You can rise above and walk in freedom from the offenses and hurts you have experienced.

There may be other things the Lord will deal with your heart to do that involves some specific areas related to your particular situation. But the following five steps still remain basic for all of us.

# STEP 1

## Accept the Fact that Forgiveness Is God's Will and Therefore It Is a Must

Forgiveness is not an optional item in our Christian life and walk. Forgiveness is essential!

Let's return to our earlier use of an automobile as an illustration of the essential must of forgiveness.

You can buy a car with or without air-conditioning. It is optional. Different types of assisted steering can also be optional as is a radio, music player, FM stereo, satellite stations, power windows, rear view cameras, GPS, power heated/cooled leather seats, sun/moon roof, tinted glass, and other perks that enrich our enjoyment of an automobile but are not essential to its primary and basic function as transportation.

However, it would be foolish to buy a car that does not have an engine. Or a transmission. Or wheels. Or a fuel tank/source and system. Or cooling system. Or brakes. All of these items, and other similar things, are ESSENTIAL to the practical and safe operation of an automobile as transportation.

Optional equipment you can do without and still have transportation. You can travel across the nation without them. Granted, your travel may not be as comfortable or stylish, but still you will be transported from point A to point B.

However, you cannot travel across the nation or anywhere else in an automobile that does not have an engine, a transmission, and the other can-not-work-without equipment. These items are not optional. They are essential.

Children can play-drive a toy car that does not have the above mentioned essentials, but the only purpose that will be served is entertainment. Children can be transported into fantasy by so doing, but fantasy is the only place that a car without the essentials is going to transport anyone!

So it is in our Christian life and walk. When we try to live without the essentials of what God's clearly revealed will is for our lives we are simply transporting ourselves into a fantasy realm. We are playing church, prayer, worship, Christian living, and the like!

Forgiveness is not an optional item in the Christian's life and walk. It is essential. It is a vital part of the will of God for every Christian. Again, as earlier, consider that the Word of God is very clear on this.

[12] "And forgive us our debts, as we forgive our debtors. [14] For if you forgive men their trespasses, your heavenly Father will also forgive you. [15] But if you do not forgive men their trespasses, neither will your Father forgive your trespasses" *(Matthew 6.12, 14–15 NKJV).*

[25] "And whenever you stand praying, if you have anything against anyone, forgive him, that your Father in heaven may also forgive you your trespasses. [26] But if you do not forgive, neither will your Father in heaven forgive your trespasses" *(Mark 11.25-26 NKJV).*

"So My heavenly Father also will do to you if each of you, from his heart, does not forgive his brother his trespasses" *(Matthew 18.35 NKJV).*

## JESUS IS CLEARLY TELLING US IF WE ARE FORGIVEN THEN WE MUST BE FORGIVING!

There are other similar passages of scriptures showing that forgiveness is essential, not optional. It is best not to tamper with what Jesus and the other Scriptures say or gamble with the outcome of His warnings. We do best to realize and accept that Jesus said what He meant and He meant what He said.

Therefore to persist in unforgiveness is folly. I do not under any circumstances want to persist in being unforgiving and wait to see if what Jesus warned us of will happen. That is foolish thinking and reasoning.

## If we are Forgiven then we must be Forgiving!

The will of our God and Heavenly Father is not optional. It is essential! Read carefully the familiar words of our Lord Jesus:

21 Not everyone who says to Me, "Lord, Lord," shall enter the kingdom of heaven, but he who does the will of My Father in heaven. 22 Many will say to Me in that day, "Lord, Lord, have we not prophesied in Your name, cast out demons in Your name, and done many wonders in Your name?" 23 And then I will declare to them, "I never knew you; depart from Me, you who practice lawlessness!" *(Matthew 7.21–23 NKJV)*

It is clearly revealed in the scriptures that forgiveness is the will of God for our lives. So I state again, forgiveness is essential, not optional.

We cannot simply call Him "Lord" and then proceed to select only those things that we want to do "in" His "name" while leaving the other essentials of His will undone and think that will be enough.

It would be like trying to use a car for transportation that had an engine and drive train but no wheels. You are not going to make it to your destination.

If there is to be a continuous flow and fullness of the Holy Spirit's presence, anointing, and ministry in our lives, homes, marriages, friendships, ministries, and churches, we must have forgiving hearts. It is an absolute essential, not an option!

Is it essential that Christ have first place and be the Lord in our lives? Then it is essential that we forgive. When we forgive we are putting Christ first in our lives because we are doing what He taught us to do *(see John 14.21, 23, & 24)*. He spoke that which the Father taught Him. He did that which He saw the Father do *(John 5.19, 30; 6.38; 7.16–17; 8.26, 28, 38)*. It is only as we continue in his Word that we are His disciples and made free by His truth *(John 8.30–32)*.

"And be kind to one another, tenderhearted, forgiving one another, just as God in Christ forgave you." *(Ephesians 4.32 NKJV)*

It was for Christ's sake that the Father has forgiven us. We are now to forgive one another even as God forgave us—that is, for Christ's sake. For His Body's sake, the Church. For the sake of each member of His Body, the believer.

Forgiveness is essential, therefore it is a must. Once this oft stated truth from God's Word grips your heart then you are ready to proceed to the second step.

# STEP 2

## COMMIT YOURSELF TO FORGIVE AS CHRIST HAS COMMANDED

All truly effective commitments we make as a Christian believer must be based on God's revealed Word and Will.

When commitment is based upon what we just emotionally feel, or upon a line of thinking that looks for the easiest and smoothest road, we enter into a gravely unstable situation. As soon as the feeling lifts or things begin to shift on us, our commitment will suddenly shift, lift, weaken, and die *(see Matthew 13.3–6, 20–21 NKJV)*.

The only successful and lasting commitment that results in true discipleship is that which is based upon believing and obeying what God has said regardless of what we feel or think at the moment.

As one of our great twentieth-century church leaders, Dr. Thomas Zimmerman, use to frequently say, "God said it and that settles it— whether I believe it or not" *(rather than just "God said it, I believe it, and that settles it")*.

> "God said it and that settles it—whether I believe it or not"

We believe and obey not because things will necessarily go better, or, it feels great and is a wonderful emotional high. We do it because Jesus said to do it. His will and word are both good and good for us. We are His. He bought us with a tremendous price *(I Peter 1.17–19)*. We are no longer our own *(I Corinthians 6.19–20)*. Therefore, we commit ourselves to doing what He has taught us because it is right in the sight of the Lord and therefore it is holy and proper.

"Blessed *are* those who hunger and thirst for righteousness, for they shall be filled" *(Matthew 5.6 NKJV)*

"But seek first the kingdom of God and His righteousness, and all these things shall be added to you" *(Matthew 6.33 NKJV)*

Never does our Lord teach us to seek good feelings, the American dream, the happiest way, what we enjoy doing, and then after these things discipleship and righteousness.

We are to seek first what is right and foremost to the heart of God. We are to do what Christ has taught us regardless of what the cost might be. We are to be a disciple *(to which the word discipline is related)* and follow Him in all things.

When doing what is right in the sight of the Lord is first on our agenda of living, then the proper feelings, the better life from above manifesting itself here below, and holy enjoyments of God's abundant living are added to us. But first things first—always!

We do not forgive just because we feel good about it or because it gives us an emotional high of some kind. We forgive because it is right in the sight of the Lord. That is what our Lord Jesus Christ said we must do.

God deliver us from being a part of any type or hype of a now-generation culture in these sinful times! How appropriate the term a now-generation is. The fallen sinful nature still cries out as did the prodigal son *"give me the portion of goods that falls to me"* Now! *(cf. Luke 15.12)*. God help us to realize that we belong to God's chosen now-generation and so commit ourselves to its reason for being as declared in the following verse of Scripture:

"But you *are* a **chosen** generation, a royal priesthood, a holy nation, His own special people, that you may proclaim the praises of Him who called you out of darkness into His marvelous light; who once *were* not a people but *are* **now** the people of God, who had not obtained mercy but **now** have obtained mercy *(I Peter 2.9–10 NKJV).*

**And as we have now obtained mercy we are now to show mercy!** God never ordained a priesthood that was not involved in mercy, forgiveness, compassion, grace, and help in the time of need! *(see Hebrews 4.14–5.3)*

How can we function as the royal priesthood of the believer in Christ and not be forgiving? How can a man be the priest of his home if he is not forgiving? A priesthood is ordained by God ultimately for the express purpose of atonement, reconciliation, and forgiveness.

No, you do not wait until it feels good, or some emotional high comes before you begin to forgive. You make a commitment to do what you know Christ teaches and says. You commit yourself to do what is right, what is truth, by meditating on it, thinking about it, putting it into your heart. Regardless of what the immediate outcome might be you commit yourself to do what is yours to do as one belonging to Christ and leave the ultimate outcome in His able and capable hands.

You commit in your heart and in your thinking. You assent with your consciousness to what Christ has said. You make yourself aware by His Word of what you must do. You purpose in your heart and you make up your mind. In your will and by God's strength you determine you will do it.

Recall once again the truth we considered earlier:

*"I can do all things through Christ who strengthens me" (Philippians 4.13 NKJV).*

Christ said to forgive, so we commit ourselves to do exactly that—we forgive! And then step 3 follows.

# STEP 3

## BEGIN NOW SPEAKING FORGIVENESS AND PERSIST IN SPEAKING IT

A significant number of years ago the Lord made real to my heart that WHAT WE SPEAK AND TALK WE KEEP AND WALK! WHAT WE THINK ABOUT AND TALK ABOUT IS WHAT WE WILL WALK OUT. We are what we predominately speak and say *(not in a secular pop-psychology sense of self-help— nor in the extreme that some have taken it in what has become known as the name it and claim it group—but in the sense that I am going to believe and agree with the report of the Lord)!*

> What we speak and talk we keep and walk! What we think about and talk about is what we will walk out.

We start by accepting that forgiveness is essential because it is the will of God and therefore we commit ourselves to be forgiving. Then we need to begin verbalizing forgiveness by talking and agreeing with what God says in His Word.

One of Israel's greatest downfalls in the wilderness was the sin of murmuring (complaining, talking doubt and unbelief, agreeing with negative reports):

"nor murmur, as some of them also murmured, and were destroyed by the destroyer" *(see I Corinthians 10.1–11 NKJV).*

Speak in faith like the example Jesus set when He said,

"Get behind me Satan!" *(Matthew 16.23; Luke 4.8 NKJV)* and "Away with you, Satan!" *(Matthew 4.10 NKJV)*

Speak and renounce audibly with your mouth Satan's works of bitterness, malice, hate, and destruction. Let satanic and demonic powers along with your sinful flesh-nature know exactly where you stand.

Speak and pray in faith to God. For example: "Lord, you are right as always. I am wrong to have unforgiveness and such in my heart. I repent. Father, I release them and that through forgiveness to you as of now. I obey your Word." Begin doing it and it will flow. The Holy Spirit and the Word will see to it!

If necessary and possible, speak to the one toward whom you feel unforgiveness: "I want things to be right between us as members of the Body of Christ *(or, as members of the sacred marriage bond, etc)*. Forgive me for being unforgiving. Let us be reconciled. I want to do what the Lord Jesus wants me to do as a believer. We must not let the enemy bring division between us..." The Holy Spirit will direct you wonderfully in this.

Talk and speak of your faith and power in the Lord. Embrace the promises God has spoken in His Word and let them become words you speak out from your mouth. Lay hold of and hang on to what God speaks to you in His still voice in your heart. Again, for example, begin audibly stating: "I forgive. This is my Father's will for my life. I release all those that I have had ought against. I no longer hold anyone or anything in my judgment but turn them over to my Lord in love and forgiveness..."

Speak your faith in God's Word when you arise in the morning, go to bed in the evening, as you are driving in your automobile, praying, or whenever and wherever you can. You will be absolutely amazed at the fresh awareness of the Lord's presence and release of spiritual power that will begin flowing and continue to increase in your life over the coming days once you begin.

Have you ever noticed the difference when you pray audibly during your prayer times compared with praying just silently in your thoughts. There is something that happens when you give the thoughts of your heart a voice of spoken words. The very atmosphere around your prayers change when they are spoken aloud—even though you are not with other people.

I believe that the words of our mouth are critical because we are made in the image of God. In the New Birth (being born-again) we take on the image of Christ. Genesis 1 states that *"GOD SAID—and it was so"* numerous times in the creation process. John 1.1–14 says that Jesus was the very Word of God made flesh and that as many as received Him to them he gave authority to become the sons of God.

Jesus said we shall give an account for every idle word that we speak *(Matthew 12.36–37)* and He warns us that wrong words that come out of our mouth defile us *(Matthew 15.16–20)*. None other of all God's creation on earth has the ability to speak, formulate languages, and write as does mankind, whom God created in His image.

To slow down mankind's sinful rebellion on earth God confused the languages at the Tower of Babel *(Genesis 11.1–9)* and when bringing mankind out of sinful rebellion there was the significance of speaking in other languages *(tongues)* on the Day of Pentecost *(Acts 2.1-11)*.

Jesus said:

"It is the Spirit who gives life; the flesh profits nothing. The **words** that I **speak** to you are **spirit**, and they are **life**" *(John 6.63 NKJV)*.

When the officers who were sent to capture Jesus and bring Him for examination were questioned as to why they had failed to do so, they replied to the leaders who had sent them,

"No man ever spoke like this Man!" *(John 7.46 NKJV)*

There are no physical descriptions of Jesus given during His earthly sojourn. We do not know the color of his hair or eyes. We do not know whether He was tall, short, or medium in height. We do not know whether He was dark or light. When Mary Magdalene encountered Him after His resurrection she did not recognize His physical appearance—but when He *spoke* her name she immediately knew Who He was *(John 20.11–18)*.

The same was true of the Emmaus disciples who, when reflecting afterwards on His post resurrection appearance to them, said,

"Did not our heart burn within us while He TALKED with us on the road, and while He opened the SCRIPTURES to us?" *(Luke 24.32 NKJV)*

Prayer involves speaking; preaching and teaching involves speaking; prophesying involves speaking; our interpersonal relationships involve speaking — and you can easily go on expanding the list!

Our speaking, talking, saying is a very critical part in our relationship and walk with the Lord. The WORD of God is one of the primary ways that God works in our lives as His people. There is so much more that could be said about words, speaking, and our mouths, but this will suffice for our purposes here. We will now proceed to step 4.

# STEP 4

## BRING ALL YOUR FORGIVENESS TALK INTO LINE WITH YOUR NEW FORGIVENESS WALK

You have seen how essential forgiveness is as the revealed will of God in His Word, the Scriptures. You have committed yourself to do it. You are now talking forgiveness. Now begin WALKING forgiveness. Bring your walk in agreement with your talk! As you talk out God's word also walk in God's Word.

God's Word says,

"And BE...forgiving." *(Ephesians 4.32)*

Bring your actions into account and accord. If that word you are about to say is not in keeping with forgiveness, then in the name of the Lord Jesus Christ swallow it! If you said it, confess your offense and repent of it. If that deed you are getting ready to do is not in keeping with the spirit of forgiveness, then for *"Christ's sake"* stifle it!

Replace the words and deeds of unforgiving bitterness and indifference with words and deeds of forgiveness that make a divine difference. This will work far more intensely than anything you can do to hush the negative suggestions of both the flesh and the devil.

Both our sinful flesh-nature and the satanic/demonic beings of darkness are going to be very reluctant to do anything that will result in a positive release of forgiveness and love in your heart and life. So every time you feel unforgiveness being stirred in you begin talking and walking forgiveness. Soon you will find those unforgiving thoughts and feelings not stirring as intensely because the enemy knows when he stirs them up that you are going to start talking and walking forgiveness even more intensely.

God has given us the authority to choose whether we will release from our life bitter or sweet water *(cf. James 3.5–11)*. We cannot do it in ourselves, but we can do all things through and in Him!

Remember, as we have discussed earlier, it is not Scripturally true to say, "I can NOT do this," when the Word of God has very emphatically declared, *"I CAN do ALL things through Christ who strengthens me" (Philippians 4.13 NKJV)*. As we have previously stated, it is no longer a question of whether we CAN, but whether we WILL or WILL NOT!

When I say to bring your walk *(behavior, attitude, actions, reactions, responses)* into line with your talk of forgiveness, I am not suggesting that you play-act forgiveness. I am talking about putting action into your talk by stepping out in a power walk to bring your actions in subjection to the will of God.

The same God Whose power will make every knee bow and every tongue confess that Jesus Christ is Lord in the Day of Judgment is at work in every Christian's life right now to make the flesh-nature bow and confess to the Lordship of Jesus Christ! *(See I John 4.4 and compare it with Philippians 2.9–11)*

I am talking about rising above unstable emotional feelings and doing a "thus says the Lord".

Forgiveness definitely takes place when you follow these steps because the Word of God is being obeyed and it will not return back to God void, empty, or unfilled. God's Word always accomplishes that which it is sent forth to do. *(See Isaiah 55.11)*

Now let's look at the final step of five.

# STEP 5

## As You Continue Forgiving, Commit It All to God and Let Him Work!

Unforgiveness is a sin problem. When we confess our sins the sins are then forgiven by God.

"If we **say** we have no sin, we deceive ourselves, and the truth is not in us. If we **confess** our sins, He is faithful and just to forgive us our sins and to cleanse us from all unrighteousness" *(I John 1.8-9 NKJV).*

The problem area is solved when we in faith leave it in the hands of God.

"Trust in the LORD with all your heart, and lean not on your own understanding; In all your ways acknowledge Him, and He shall direct your paths" *(Proverbs 3.5-6 NKJV).*

"Commit your way to the LORD, trust also in Him, and He shall bring *it* to pass" *(Psalm 37.5 NKJV).*

The Scriptures Mark 11.22-26 in the opening of this Section 6 says in effect:

1.   Speak with faith and it shall be.

2.   Pray with faith and we will have it.

3.   Forgive with faith and it is forgiven (and we are too!).

As with any sin or problem, once we have brought it to God and have done what we have been Scripturally enjoined to do there is nothing else we are or can do but leave it in the hands of God. He will take it from there.

**A POSSIBLE POINT OF CONFUSION.** I believe that here it might be well in passing to touch on a very crucial and confusing situation that arises in many hearts.

There are times when we may be shaken by a condition in which unforgiveness and forgiveness seem to be resident within us at the same time. One rises, it seems, while the other falls, and then it reverses itself. This continues going back and forth, back and forth.

This situation is due to the fact that unforgiveness is a work or a fruit of the sinful-nature while forgiveness is a fruit of the spiritual-nature resulting from the nine-fold Fruit of the Holy Spirit *(Galatians 5.22-26)* working in our spirits.

When we release within our hearts forgiveness from our spiritual-nature we immediately have a life giving flow of God's power that begins to grow His fruit in our lives, and in that very instance, the fruit of unforgiveness begins to die.

During the time that the fruit of forgiveness is growing and the fruit of un-forgiveness is dying you may sense both being present, and in a unique way they are. But there is a vast difference between the two in that presence. One is growing, expanding, and enriching while the other is dying, withering, and withdrawing from our life.

This entire situation serves again to illustrate why feelings are unstable. In every believer there is a sinful or flesh-nature and a spiritual-nature. The flesh-nature is being subdued awaiting the day of resurrection when the body will be renewed by a physical resurrection just as the spiritual nature has already been renewed by a spiritual resurrection in the new birth *(John 5.24-29; Ephesians 2.1–10; Romans 8.1–13; 12.1-2).*

We put the works (fruit) of the flesh to death through the Holy Spirit in our walk with Christ while the spiritual man is being renewed and growing stronger.

See Galatians 5, Romans 7-8, II Corinthians 4.16–18 and Romans 6.12 for some of the Scriptural background on the things we have just discussed about the works (fruit) of the flesh and spirit. A good study-reference Bible should lead you on to other Scriptures as well.

We conclude this section with a question and the answer.

## Do the Dynamics of Forgiveness that We are Writing of Really Work?

## Yes They Do!

Whenever and wherever I have been entrusted and blessed by the Lord with the opportunities to share these messages in public meetings such as a conference, special event, weekly service, Sunday services, and such we have never failed to hear exciting and truly amazing testimonies of results.

In addition to the verbal testimonies there are letters and e-mails I receive from different ones that were in attendance where I spoke and/or from the reading of the book. We are expecting even greater things from the expanded and updated printing of this book!

Let me share a few of numerous testimonies. These may sound small in comparison to many bigger needs in this area. We do have some other very great and powerful testimonies that we could share, but for concern of some recognizing who the people involved are I refrain from doing so.

However, to me, one of the things that reveals the greatness of God is how God can and does take to heart the small things as well as the big ones.

The most powerful people among us can only handle a few big problems. In contrast, God's greatness is seen in how God can handle all problems—big and small—and give the attention and provision that is needed to everyone.

**TESTIMONY ONE.** The Sunday morning that I, for the first time, ministered the sixth message of six from *The Dynamics of Forgiveness* on *How to Forgive*, there was present in the service a man who had a very successful ministry. This was his first service under our ministry.

He was not ministering extensively at that time. Although he was a man still in the prime of his years several serious problems of health and church opposition had necessitated him stepping out of his ministry at the time.

In his most recent pastorate, as he shared in his testimony that he personally related to me, something had happened that put him in a bad light with some members of his church concerning a legal matter of which he feels he was innocent.

A group of these members had taken a negative stand against him. Opposition increased. Offenses occurred. Feelings of unforgiveness developed. The binding came and there was no resolve forthcoming for the situation. He then resigned and left the church as the pastor.

This had happened, as I have said, just a brief while before he and his family began attending our church. After hearing this message that Sunday morning on *How to Forgive* he went home.

At home he asked the Holy Spirit to direct him in removing all areas of unforgiveness from his life. He began to think about the group of people at his former pastorate, and what they had said about him and done to him and vice-versa. He then began to release them through forgiveness before the Throne of God in the privacy of his home (that is, in One-Way Forgiveness we spoke of earlier).

That very week, in just a matter of a few days, he saw a van drive up in front of his residence. His eyes grew wide as he saw the very group of people involved in the offenses previously mentioned step out of the van. They came and knocked on the door. He opened the door. They came in and sat down.

Why were they there? They were not exactly sure. *Something*, they said, had got hold of each of their hearts that very week and impressed them they should come and see this minister. They had not seen him since his resigning as the pastor of their church. As the meeting went on forgiveness was forthcoming, apologies were made, and resolve came!

Why? You will never convince me (nor that minister) this was just a coincidence. Similar things and testimonies like this happen time and again when these messages of forgiveness are presented and acted upon. When that minister began to confess the sin of his bitter feelings of hurt and unforgiveness toward these people, he released himself, them, and heaven by forgiveness. The Holy Spirit then began to immediately work. Release and holy resolve was the result.

**TESTIMONY TWO.** When the Lord suddenly imparted these forgiveness truths to my heart I was totally unaware that a man in our pastorate at the time had electronically bugged my home.

He had a background in high-tech security work and had been hired for his expertise by some very well known people in the entertainment industry. Our pastorate at the time was located in the outlying area of Hollywood and Burbank where many of the very talented personalities in both acting and music lived.

He would later tell me that he had not only electronically bugged our home, but had done the same to a few others who attended the church—primarily those in places of leadership and influence.

He made recordings of the conversations he heard from my home (bedrooms, living areas, kitchen, etc). He would then engage me in conversation and ask questions about things that he already knew what I truly thought and at times I had commented on in the privacy of my home. He did the same with others whose homes he had bugged. A scripture comes to my mind when I think about this.

Never make light of the king, even in your thoughts. And don't make fun of the powerful, even in your own bedroom. For a little bird might deliver your message and tell them what you said. *(Ecclesiastes 10.20 NLT)*

I am so very thankful that I was honest in my answers to him. In the areas where I felt that he was not the one with whom the matter should be discussed I was honest in telling him that as well.

This had gone on for a considerable time up to the time I sold that particular home and purchased a condominium. And I did not know it. Neither did the others that he was doing the same to.

Then came the day when the Lord released me to begin the series of messages on *The Dynamics of Forgiveness* for the first time. This was after I had first made applications of them to my own life. There were six messages which basically correspond to the first six sections of this book.

God moved very powerfully and deeply in those services. The Holy Spirit's convicting work in people's hearts and minds was profound. People were broken in heart and began repenting of the bitterness, hate, anger, and the like in their hearts toward others in their life, home, family, marriage, business, and church.

Among the many people God began this forgiveness work in was the man who had bugged my home. Following those services he met with me privately. He wept and confessed what he had done to my home and the homes of others in the church. He brought the recordings asking for forgiveness. The recordings were appropriately destroyed and forgiveness along with reconciliation forth coming.

He became one of the greatest encouragers of my ministry from that day forward and very instrumental in this forgiveness message going out on a much larger scale other than just our local church.

This outcome remains to this day one of greatest divine miracles of life and personality transformations that I have personally ever witnessed—and I have seen God do some great works in this area since it seems that this is one of the primary ways that God has chosen to use my ministry.

Yes! Forgiveness works. Forgiveness can be one of the most single essential things that you can do to see God work powerfully in your life as you let go of and release all the debts that you feel others owe to you along with all the bitterness, anger, and like that has come into your heart as a result of offenses.

**TESTIMONY THREE.** There was a young husband and wife in one of our pastorates before I became the pastor of the church where I received and first preached this forgiveness message series.

The couple was very active in the church and loved the Lord. Their family included two children. While we were there the young lady became pregnant with her and her husband's third child. The Lord gave my wife a unique prophetic word concerning the child (which was not a typical thing for my wife to do). The child was born and the prophetic word my wife gave proved to be truly from the Lord (for which my wife was very relieved and thankful).

Our pastoral ministry continued on. Then one day my District Superintendent phoned me and said the Lord had put me on his heart for a church. I consented to pray about it and, although I did not want to leave where I was, I went and ministered at the church my superintendent had contacted me about. The Lord spoke to my heart to accept the church's invitation to come as their new pastor.

Consequently considerable time went by and we lost contact with the young couple and their sweet family.

Then the Lord imparted this forgiveness message to my heart. And then shortly after that we felt directed of the Lord to pastor a church in northwest

Arkansas where these messages were made into a book and began to circulate in all directions as I never envisioned it doing.

The book came into the hands of this young lady now a significant number of years later. I was not aware at the time someone had given her a copy for we had lost contact with the couple and their family.

And another thing I did not know was that she and her husband had divorced. They had been divorced approximately five years when she got the book and read it. God began His great work of grace, forgiveness began flowing, and after five or so years of being divorced the couple remarried. They later went into the ministry and became pastors.

What a great God we serve! The enemy of our souls just cannot prevail when we walk in the power and grace of our God!

**TESTIMONY FOUR.** This testimony was sent to me by a lady who contacted me to see about purchasing another book to replace one she had given away. I never met the woman nor the man to whom she had given her copy of my book.

The man she had given the book to was a concert pianist she had met during an air flight that was taking him to one his concerts. This woman who had obtained a copy of my book happened to be seated next to him.

They engaged in conversation. The gentlemen began sharing some great heartaches he was going through and things that had happened in which he was offended and hurt.

Before the flight was completed the lady shared what God had done in her life as a result of forgiveness. She gave him the copy of my book she had.

He had time to begin reading and then continued reading before that evening of his concert. God poured His grace and love into the man's heart. He surrendered His life to the Lordship of Christ. The forgiveness that flowed from God's throne into his heart now began to work forgiveness toward those who had grievously offended him.

God did such a work in his life that he contacted the lady who had given him the book to tell her his testimony of what God had done and how he had shared at his concert that night about the release and freedom forgiveness can work in a person's life.

Yes! Forgiveness works. And it will work for you as it has for so many others through the years. You do not have to go through life bitter, angry, hating, unhappy, bound, and being eaten up. Forgive. Let go. Let God.

**TESTIMONY FIVE.** The very week that the Holy Spirit, I feel, imparted these messages to my heart I began talking and speaking forgiveness before the Throne of God's grace in the One-Way Forgiveness. This was before I even brought one of the messages publicly because the Lord had indicated to me that I was to set forgiveness in place in my own life before bringing any forgiveness messages to any congregation.

There was one couple in our pastorate at this time who had deeply offended my wife and me. And we had deeply offended them. I had begun to earnestly speak and pray forgiveness toward them during the above mentioned time.

There was no fellowship between us and them *(how could there be?)* at the time I began speaking and praying forgiveness.

I cannot go into all the details here because there are those that would then know of whom I was speaking. I do not want to cause any embarrassment from a beautiful resolve that is nothing less than the work of the Holy Spirit in the very thing that I have been speaking of throughout this book. Suffice it to be said it had been an extremely delicate and painful situation.

I spoke and embraced forgiveness before the Lord for the offenses they had done against us. I repented of the ill feelings that I had allowed to enter my own heart and asked the Lord to forgive me for my offenses to them and Him.

Now there were still quite a few occasions where we would see this couple in public. When those occasions occurred any words spoken were quite forced from all of us. I believe it is called civil politeness. Sometimes there were no words at all, especially when there did not have to be (actually, there are times when being quiet can be civil politeness!).

Within a matter of a week and a few days after this time of speaking, praying, repenting, and embracing forgiveness (again private and the One-Way Forgiveness) this couple was present in a gathering where we all were at. When they saw us there they purposely came to my wife and me and hugged our necks! All of us visited together for awhile and they told us they loved us!

When my wife and I got home we were, as some would say, flabbergasted! That is, we were stunned and shocked. We could not believe it. Afterward as my wife and I began to reflect on the evening's unusual turn of events the conversation between my wife and I went something like this: "Did you see what happened!? Honey, I cannot believe it! I wonder what they are up to…!!??!"

*"O fools, and slow of heart to believe"* (cf. Luke 24.25). We both went to bed that night like Nebuchadnezzar of old when Daniel told him, *"thoughts came to your mind while on your bed, about what would come to pass after this"* (cf. Daniel 2.29).

The next morning when I awoke, that still, small voice of the Lord spoke in my heart: "Did you not commit the situation involving this couple to me? Did you not release them to My help and to My care? Did you not forgive them and ask forgiveness for yourself?"

Then I remembered my forgiveness sessions with the Lord just about a week or so before. Excited, I called to my wife and told her, "Honey, do you know what happened last night with _____ and _____? I released them a few days ago through forgiveness and God has worked to bring resolve to pass!"

That was not the end of the matter. It was just a glorious opener. A few days later we received a Christmas card from them. This was the Christmas following the Thanksgiving week-end when God first and suddenly started pouring these truths into my heart. And it was before I publically preached the messages for the very first time. It made my Christmas. The card was a beautiful picture of their family with the usual season's greetings printed on it, but there was a special notation they had written to us. This is what it said:

"Have a wonderful Christmas. We really love you folks, and hope God really blesses you in_____. Hope you'll forgive us if we might have caused you any problems. We love you. Signed _____."

What a mighty and fascinating God we serve! How mighty His Word is in fulfillment! My spirit soared. I discovered that these dynamics of forgiveness really work. Forgiveness does loose situations that seem absolutely hopeless of any resolve. Miracles of grace occur when the Holy Spirit is loosed to work by forgiveness! But they are very limited where He is bound by unforgiveness.

How we need this revelation! Preachers need it. Church members need it. Husbands need it. Wives need it. Parents need it. Children need it. You need it. I need it. Everyone needs it.

## AN IMAGE OF HORROR AND THE GOD OF HOPE

As I stood there re-reading this couple's Christmas card to us an image formed in my mind and I could see a dreadful creature with tentacles, resembling those coming from of an octopus, entwining churches everywhere throughout our nation, along with homes, marriages, and lives. I could see multitudes dying and struggling to be free, but they remained bound! They could not see the tentacles that held them and were crushing the life from their churches, homes, marriages, and lives.

I could feel myself crying out, "O God, how can these horrible and countless number of twisted and knotted tentacles be unraveled? Where is there a deliverance from such seemingly hopeless situations?" Then the Holy Spirit, I feel, whispered to my heart, "These are the problems, misunderstandings, hurts, offenses, and disillusionments that are too hopelessly complex for human reasoning and solutions. Forgiveness is the only way that these tentacles of destruction that are entwined around these lives and places can be broken and dissolved so that My healing and restoration can come!"

My heart cries that I will always be a person of forgiveness. Never again do I want to merely learn to live with something or just miserably put up with it and go on. I want to forgive. Completely, wholly, and totally. Only then can the Holy Spirit be loosed to fully work in bringing about a definite resolve to the hopelessly entangled situations that bind renewal and our desperately needed continuing outpourings of the Holy Spirit.

## FORGIVENESS IS GOD'S ULTIMATE WAY OF DEALING WITH OFFENSES.

For many who find they themselves bound, deeply entwined, and hopelessly entangled in these very situations it is the only way and solution. Enter into your priesthood ministry. Release a continuous flow of forgiveness from your life. Then behold all God can and will do for and through you.

## YOU CAN FORGIVE IF YOU WILL!

# THOUGHTS

When we commit ourselves to truly follow our Lord by obedient faith to His Word powerful things happen in our heart, mind, and life.

We were writing earlier of the power of words and actions in coming against the attacks of satanic/demonic powers that seek to distract, isolate, and destroy us.

The Master of Distraction, Satan, will seek to divert our attention by using people even as he endeavored to use Peter against Christ.

Try this. When someone becomes a distraction to you in any way begin praying for them. Pray that God will work mightily in their lives. That His Kingdom and will comes and is done in and through them. Pray for their lives to be blessed with God's joy unspeakable and His peace that passes all understanding. Pray that God gives them wisdom to make choices that will bring God's very best to their lives.

I don't care if it is someone that irritates you or someone who intrigues and interests you and that you may become wrongly attracted to. You will find when you do this and pray for them that the satanic/demonic forces of darkness will over time stop using them as a distraction to you. Satan is not going to continue using anyone or anything that causes you to begin earnestly praying for others well being.

# QUESTIONS

1. What is the significance for you in Step 1: Accept the Fact That Forgiveness is God's Will and Therefore It Is A Must?

2. What is the significance for you in Step 2: Commit Yourself to Forgive As Christ Has Commanded?

3. What is the significance for you in Step 3: Begin Now Speaking Forgiveness and Persist In Speaking It?

4. What is the significance for you in Step 4: Bring All Your Forgiveness Talk Into Line with Your New Forgiveness Walk?

5. What is the significance for you in Step 5: As You Continue Forgiving Commit It All to God and Let Him Work?

6. Does forgiveness work? Why? How? When?

7. Will you let forgiveness work in your life?

8. In Thoughts what does the author discuss that may have significance for you?

# Section Seven

## PART 1 OF 3
## THREE OBSTACLES TO OBTAINING
## WHAT GOD HAS FOR YOU

### Obstacle One

### The Grind of Time and
### The Weight of Waiting

# MATTHEW 14.22–36 (NASB95)

## (ALSO MARK 6.41-52; JOHN 6.11-21)

²² Immediately He *[*Jesus]* made the disciples get into the boat and go ahead of Him to the other side, while He sent the crowds away.

²³ After He had sent the crowds away, He went up on the mountain by Himself to pray; and when it was evening, He was there alone.

²⁴ But the boat was already a long distance from the land, battered by the waves; for the wind was contrary.

²⁵ And in the fourth watch of the night He came to them, walking on the sea.

²⁶ When the disciples saw Him walking on the sea, they were terrified, and said, "It is a ghost!" And they cried out in fear.

²⁷ But immediately Jesus spoke to them, saying, "Take courage, it is I; do not be afraid."

²⁸ Peter said to Him, "Lord, if it is You, command me to come to You on the water."

²⁹ And He said, "Come!" And Peter got out of the boat, and walked on the water and came toward Jesus.

³⁰ But seeing the wind, he became frightened, and beginning to sink, he cried out, "Lord, save me!"

³¹ Immediately Jesus stretched out His hand and took hold of him, and said to him, "You of little faith, why did you doubt?"

³² When they got into the boat, the wind stopped.

³³ And those who were in the boat worshiped Him, saying, "You are certainly God's Son!"

³⁴ When they had crossed over, they came to land at Gennesaret.

³⁵ And when the men of that place recognized Him, they sent *word* into all that surrounding district and brought to Him all who were sick;

³⁶ and they implored Him that they might just touch the fringe of His cloak; and as many as touched *it* were cured. *[* ] author's insertion*

# Are You Among Those Who Feel that the Promises of God Work for Some But Not for Others?

## And Do You Feel That You May Be One of Those Others but Not One of the Some?

I had another Saturday experience in 1988 a bit similar to the one I had in 1975 (although the intensity and complexity was on a smaller scale).

On an August 20, 1988 Saturday morning during breakfast the following truths began to unexpectedly fill my heart and thinking on obstacles we all will face and have to overcome in order to obtain the fullness of God's promises in our lives.

I have since shared these truths in a series of three messages to great effect in numerous states, pastorates, and special services as a guest speaker.

I am including these truths in this enlarged and revised edition of *The Dynamics of Forgiveness* because it deals with three basic obstacles that all of us have to face and rise above if we want to see the fullness of God's spiritual and supernatural work in any area of our lives.

This includes seeing God work in us as I have shared in this book in the various areas of the dynamics of forgiveness (although, as I just said, these three truths readily apply to all areas of our life encounters as well). So I ask you the following questions:

Do you feel you have obtained all that God has for you up to this point of time in your life? Many of us don't.

Do you want to obtain a greater fullness of all God has for you in the upcoming days of your life? Most of us do.

Do you want to see God do for you what you have seen Him do in and for others? Most of us desire this.

Do you want to see God's dynamics of forgiveness bring that break through turn around in your life in stopping the deep offenses of hurt before they stop you? If you have read to this point in the book I believe you do.

I invite you to look with fresh eyes at one of the most well know events in the life of Christ on earth—His walking on the waters of a raging storm and His call and commitment to Peter to do the same.

# THE PROCESS OF TIME

[22] Immediately He made the disciples get into the boat and go ahead of Him to the other side, while He sent the crowds away *[immediately after the feeding of the 5,000].
[23] After He had sent the crowds away, He went up on the mountain by Himself to pray; and when it was evening, He was there alone.
[24] But the boat was already a long distance from the land, battered by the waves; for the wind was contrary. *(Matthew 14.22-24 NASB95)*   *[ ] are the author's addition to the text

**Life for all of us involves a process of time** whose steady flow and currents carry us from our beginnings to our certain end—and all the points in between. I have heard this referred to as the dash on a tombstone between the date we are born and the date we die. This dash or process of time lasts longer for some than it does for others, but it is a reality for all of us.

This ever moving process of time in each of our lives is made up of differing seasons and events.

TO EVERYTHING there is a season, and a time for every matter *or* purpose under heaven: *(Ecclesiastes 3.1 Amplified Bible)*

[5] ... And a wise man's heart discerns both time and judgment,
[6] Because for every matter there is a time and judgment ... *(Ecclesiastes 8.5-6 NKJV)*

The Gospel of John tells us that this incident recorded in Matthew 14 was at a time in our Lord's life that had come when the people, after experiencing the miraculous feeding of the five thousand, wanted to come and make Him their king. Jesus knowing this and knowing that this was not the time in the will of His Father for Him to become King made His disciples get into a boat to leave the area and the crowd action that was developing. He then, quietly slipped away and went up on the mountainside to pray *(John 6.14-15)*.

Time was one of the areas that Jesus' disciples struggled with. In the Old Testament God had spoken of coming times when Israel would see their nation's national glory restored to a greater height than ever before. Jesus' arrival and manifestations seemed to be a part of God fulfilling those times. And yet, Jesus' timing confused them as His ministry seemed to be moving in an opposite direction.

Based on the prophetic teachings circulating in Judah in the disciple's day they too, like the multitude that Jesus had just miraculously fed, were expectant and even insistent on occasions that the Kingdom was going to appear when Jesus reached Jerusalem. Consequently they were disturbed when Jesus talked about His approaching suffering and dying.

Even after His resurrection when Jesus was giving the disciples some of the their final instructions just before ascending back to the Father the disciples were still asking about the time of His rule and reign as the Messiah King of Israel:

> [6] Therefore, when they had come together, they asked Him, saying, "Lord, will You at this time restore the kingdom to Israel?"
> [7] And He said to them, "It is not for you to know times or seasons which the Father has put in His own authority." *(Acts 1.6-8 NKJV)*

The disciples had made some serious miscalculations about time and seasons which resulted in them becoming confused as they tried to hold Jesus to their time schedule instead of living and walking in His.

Time is still one of the great struggles for Jesus' followers today. One of the greatest obstacles in our walk with God is the fact we are a time-orientated people serving a God Who ordains eternity. We are a people who see life as it is right now serving a God Who sees our life from the beginning to the end — and eternally beyond. We are a people who struggle to give the eternal God the time of day much less the entirety of time in our brief life span.

We have a problem with properly handling time — as did Abraham and Sarah during the twenty-five years from the promise of a child until the birth of Isaac. It was the mishandling of time between when God first promised them a child and the day that Isaac was born which resulted in an Ishmael being born that would later become a grief to Sarah and a heart break for Abraham.

In their eyes it looked like time had passed them by, but time never truly passes the eternal purposes of God by. Time only passes by our concepts of God's purposes and work in our lives. Abraham and Sarah's mishandling of time resulted in them and their descendents being unnecessarily mishandled by the times through the coming years.

Waiting on God involves time and that involves the millstone of time grinding out the refining process of separating the wheat from the chaff.

Time seems to move painfully slow when we want or feel that we need something now. We grow impatient and nervous and are in danger of jumping the proverbial gun during what appears to be time standing still (which time never does!).

Over the lengthy years of my life I have learned a great truth. Time and truth always walk hand-in-hand together. Time will always confirm the truth—and expose the lie. Time is always on the side of truth and truth is always on the side of time. Time is always against untruth or the lie. And untruth or the lie is always against time. And all of our times our firmly in the hands of God.

> **Time and truth always walk hand-in-hand together.**

## THE PROTRACTION OF TIME

We are consumed with a hurried and rushed sense of time. In the USA and most of the industrialized world we are constantly working to make things happen faster and better in less and less time. We want things now. We want to be there now. We want to know it now. We want to have it now.

Where the real time strain comes for us is in our perception of a protraction of time that seems like it will never end. At least not end well.

Try to imagine what it must have been like for the disciples of Jesus out on the sea in the midst of the threatening turbulence of the wind and waves threshing both them and their boat while Jesus is up on the mountain side praying. The winds become stronger, the waves become higher, and the shore seems farther away than ever before.

The last time their boat was caught in a storm on this sea Jesus was in it with them. He had arisen and told the wind to "Be quiet!" And the wind and waves had instantly stopped and they were safe *(Mark 4.35-41)*.

But Jesus was not in the boat with them this time. He was up on the mountainside praying—and, unknown to them, He saw their struggles in the storm about 4 to 5 miles from the shore line.

When you are in a crisis-time seconds seem like minutes and minutes feel like hours.

A few friends and myself took a boat I had out on the Salton Sea in the Imperial Valley on the lower desert of Southern California during the dark hours after midnight one Sunday evening after services. Southern California is very much like Israel's topography from the coast and mountains to the desert. The Sea was somewhere around 270 feet below sea level surrounded by hills and mountainous terrain. The Sea of Galilee is around 600 feet below sea level and surrounded by mountainous terrain.

There was very little to no light in this particular harbor area where we chose to put the boat into the calm waters of the bay. Things were fine until we got out just beyond the mouth of the smooth harbor waters.

Suddenly the boat began dropping as it suddenly plunged in between turbulent waves that had unexpectedly come up along with a sudden and steadily growing wind. The boat began taking on water as I began to slowly and carefully get the boat facing into the waves while making what seemed like a large and endless half circle to get back into the protected and calmer waters of the harbor.

It was only a matter of about 15 or 20 minutes but it felt like literally hours. It was a horrifying experience.

I have been in several strong earthquakes. They generally last only 10 to 15 seconds but it feels like forever. I have been through several tornadoes where minutes felt like hours. When stressful or threatening situations occur time becomes very protracted to our senses.

And when time feels protracted the grind of time and the weight of waiting begin to grow unbearable.

## THE PUZZLE OF TIME

Against time's backdrop the events of our lives can appear to our narrow perspective like getting pieces of a puzzle a few at a time that we do not have a picture for. But all the pieces of the puzzle of time and our life are in God's hands—and He has the complete picture and knows where every piece goes and fits together.

[47] Now when evening came, the boat was in the middle of the sea; and He *was* alone on the land.
[48] Then He saw them straining at rowing, for the wind was against them. Now about the fourth watch of the night He came to them, walking on the sea ... *(Mark 6.47-48 NKJV)*

Today Jesus our Savior is at the right hand of the Father in heaven praying and interceding on our behalf *(Romans 8.28-39 note verse 34)*. Our Savior sees and watches over us in all the times and seasons of our lives. When the storms descend He sees and He knows. And He will come to us—even if it is in the fourth watch of our lives. In truth, He never leaves us or forsakes and He is with us to the end of the age itself *(Matthew 28.20; Hebrews 13.5)*.

The fourth watch was between 3: to 6:a.m. We all know that can be the deadest, darkest, and most unnerving time of the night hours. It is the final hours of night and dark. It is a time when problems always appear larger than they are, when sickness feels more deadly than it is, and when we feel that sunrise is never going to come. But the sunrise always follows the fourth watch (and sometimes comes right at the closing of the fourth watch itself).

We must rise above the obstacle of the grind of time and the weight of waiting in order to see the great things God will do for us in the process, protraction, and puzzle of time.

Our walk with the Lord is not a one hundred yard dash or a sixty second sprint. It is a life time marathon. You will never know the God Who comes to you walking on the water until you rise above the obstacle of time.

As it has been widely and wisely observed, you cannot wait in a hurry—that is a contradiction. Time is the essence of all great works, art, and accomplishments. You do not get an educational degree of worth and value in a month or a year. You do not become an expert in a particular line of work without the investment and wise use of much time. Money does not compound by interest from a small investment into a great provision over night or even in a few years.

Mark the men and women you have seen God do great works of His presence in. They are men and women who have learned to wait on God and thus have risen above the grind of time and the weight of waiting into the fullness of God's eternal workings.

God is making all things work together for good to them that love Him and are called according to His purpose *(Romans 8.28)*. The backdrop of time is explicitly implied as a distinct part of the process in that promise that all things are working together for good. Don't jump ship and drown. He is taking you from the place where He comes walking on the water to where you are now to take you to the place where more of His glory will be seen and lives changed.

When God puts you in a boat with instructions to cross over to the other side you must spend as much time in the boat as it takes to reach the other side. To see what God has for you and will do for you next you have to stay where God puts you now until He tells you different. Otherwise you will never see all that God has in His heart and will do for you in the dash between your birth and departure.

Let God turn the crushing stones of time into stepping stones of timeliness and timelessness in your life.

But they that wait upon the LORD shall renew *their* strength; they shall mount up with wings as eagles; they shall run, and not be weary; *and* they shall walk, and not faint. *(Isaiah 40.31 KJV)*

They may even walk on the water. For sure, they will reach the next place God has ordained for them in His time-line of life and divine design.

# QUESTIONS

1.  How are you handling the process of time that is happening in your life up to this point in your God given time-line?

2.  Are there things you need to be doing significantly different in how you handle the times of your life? How will you implement these needed changes?

3.  Does a sense of the protraction of time stop you very often from waiting and staying in the place God has placed you until you know He has completed his work in your life for that time period?

4.  What are the most troubling things about time for you? And what can you do to lower the intensity of these troubling areas?

5.  What is meant by today's saying, "You cannot wait in a hurry"?

6.  What did the Lord mean by the word "wait" in Isaiah 30.41? Reflect on this. Remember, we call someone who serves us a "waiter" or "waitress". Why do we use these terms for them?

# SECTION SEVEN

## PART 2 OF 3
## THREE OBSTACLES TO OBTAINING
## WHAT GOD HAS FOR YOU

### OBSTACLE TWO

### THE UNNATURAL OF THE SUPERNATURAL

# THE UN-NATURAL OF TODAY'S NATURAL

<sup>25</sup> And in the fourth watch of the night He came to them, walking on the sea.
<sup>26</sup> When the disciples saw Him walking on the sea, they were terrified, and said, "It is a ghost!" And they cried out in fear.
<sup>27</sup> But immediately Jesus spoke to them, saying, "Take courage, it is I; do not be afraid."
<sup>28</sup> Peter said to Him, "Lord, if it is You, command me to come to You on the water."
<sup>29</sup> And He said, "Come!" And Peter got out of the boat, and walked on the water and came toward Jesus. *(Matt. 14.25-29 NASB95)*

**Today what is considered natural or normal was at one time unnatural and abnormal** when God first created our world. When man, through his free will, chose another source for his information, instructions, and life other than God he sinned. Sin means to miss God's mark, to fall below the life line set by God, to reject God's way and go our own way *(Romans 3.23; Isaiah 53.6)*.

When sin came into the world it brought with it an ungodly perversion and defilement that turned the natural function and beauty of God's creation into that which was unnatural and against the original nature of God's design and intent.

Sin turned the natural order of God's peace, joy, life, health, innocence, purity, harmony, beauty, and the like into turmoil, dissatisfaction, sickness, death, guiltiness, defilement, ugliness, violence, and disorder.

All of us are born into a world that is unnatural by God's standards. Our present world is upside down in contrast to what is right side up with God. It is moving toward what is destructive versus what is constructive in the Lord. Today's world is pathetically limited by living in unbelief, darkness, for the moment, and seeing only the physical/material side of creation rather than living in belief, light, fullness, while seeing both the physical/material side of creation and the spiritual side from whence all creation came *(Hebrews 11.1 & 3)*.

Before Christ comes into our lives we see only the unnatural and the upside down conception of existence. We have lived in the unnatural so long and so blindly that we presently think of what is natural to God and His Kingdom as being unnatural, supernatural, and impossible, weird and spooky, creepy and frightening.

When you have been born and raised in what is unnatural and that is all you have ever known then by default the unnatural becomes natural to you and anything else becomes, among other things, unnatural or supernatural.

When anything goes from a higher standard to a lower standard over an extended period of time then the lower standard can easily become the new norm of expectation. The higher standard or benchmark is no longer the norm—the lower standard and mark is.

If you do not have any true reference to know what is natural versus unnatural then again by default the unnatural becomes natural. This is one of the primary reasons that Satan and fallen mankind hate the Bible. The Bible shows you that the spiritual and supernatural, in a unique sense, is natural and God's norm thus exposing that which is unnatural and abnormal because of sin.

One of the great dilemmas of psychology is answering the question of what is normal or natural human behavior? You cannot know what abnormal behavior is until you know what normal behavior is.

And one of the great dilemmas and questions of philosophy is what is real, or, what is truth? One of the primary purposes philosophy serves is to make one aware of what the great questions of life are, but not necessarily to provide one with the answers; only the considerations and the possibilities.

And this is where the dilemma over the Person and Gospel of Jesus Christ comes in for fallen and sinful mankind and is expressed in the words of those who were anti-Christ in their attitude toward the preaching of the Gospel and the work of Christ through His Church:

... "These who have TURNED THE WORLD UPSIDE DOWN have come here too."
*(Acts 17.6 NKJV) Note: the ALL CAPITAL words are added by the author*

Jesus and His disciples through the ages have not been turning the world upside down—but right side up. When a person owes more money on a house or a car than either is worth on the market they are considered and called "upside down" in it. When the debt is paid down to where it is worth more than market value a person is considered "right side up".

Christ paid completely all the debt of sin owed by us to God when He took our sins on Himself and died in our place on the Cross. When we believe, repent, and surrender our life to Christ as our Lord and Savior our upside down condition in sin is completely satisfied in the courts of heaven and we become right side up in Christ.

Jesus also referred to this dilemma of not being able to see the spiritual in the midst of the physical now as well as not being able to see it in the sense of eternally entering into it when He said:

> [3] Most assuredly, I say to you, unless one is born again, he cannot SEE the kingdom of God.
> [6] That which is born of the flesh is flesh, and that which is born of the Spirit is spirit.
> [7] Do not marvel that I said to you, "You must be born again." *(John 3.3, 6-7 NKJV)*
> *Note: The CAPITAL letters added by author*

As we have indicated several times now in this book there is that something in each person of mankind that tells us there is something more than just what we see with the physical eye and hear with the physical ear. This is because God has planted an eternity-consciousness in the human heart *(Ecclesiastes 3.11 cf. Romans 1.19-20)*. And even though that consciousness has been greatly dulled by sin it arises from time to time in a pulling and pushing, nagging and nudging way at various times, seasons, and places in our lives.

A leading Bible teacher in his video series from the 1980's on the holiness of God stated that he felt that the otherness of God, or, because God is other than we are and has put that otherness awareness in us, is one of the reasons that so many are drawn to fantasy or horror type ghost and spirit themed stories and movies. They are pulled toward the sense of this otherness something or another while not comprehending what it really is.

There is this yearning and churning in us for that otherness beyond just the mundane physical. There is this ambiguous, nebulous awareness that there has to be something more. One of the memorable blues songs in the latter quarter of the twentieth century, sang by Peggy Lee contained the theme, *"Is this all there is?"* At times there is that stirring in us of that something beyond just the unnatural natural we have become nurtured and neutered in. There is this something in our 'knower' that awakens that sense of otherness—something spiritual.

But when we are confronted with that spiritual otherness breaking through sin's imposed physical barriers of unbelief and dullness we can be frightened and even terrified by it.

# THE UN-NATURAL OF THE SUPERNATURAL

## WALKING ON WATER

The disciples were terrified and screamed out in great fear, "It is a ghost!", when Jesus came walking on the water near to where they were struggling against the storm winds and waters that were battering their boat some four or so miles from the shore in the deadest and darkest hour of the night.

They had seen Jesus do some very incredible things from healing the sick, raising the dead, opening the eyes of the blind and ears of the deaf, turning water into wine, feeding 5,000 men plus women and children from a few biscuit size pieces of bread and sardine sized fish—but this was so far beyond the natural they were accustomed to that it was unnatural even as the supernatural.

In the other supernatural miracles, healings, and the like it was just different. Though it did not happen often in their day still there were people that recovered from illnesses when treated by a physician. There were those recoveries after extended times of convalescing when healing somehow worked unseen in the body. Jesus' miracles and works of the supernatural in the areas of healings and the like were at least closer to what they had witnessed in the so-called natural of their lives.

But someone walking on top of the waters in calm weather much less while winds were blowing and waves were churning was just unthinkable, unimaginable, unexplainable, and well—super-unnatural.

# THE UN-NATURAL OF THE SUPERNATURAL

## THE RIGHT-NOW AND THE "I AM"

The Right-Now for the disciples was being in a boat during a severe storm in an eerie hour of the night and the impossibility of someone walking around on top of water in the midst of the waves and wind.

But instantly He spoke to them, saying, Take courage! I AM! Stop being afraid!
*(Matthew 14.27 Amplified Bible)*

Jesus called to them to "Take courage! Be of good cheer! Do not be afraid! It is I!" Why? Because it was indeed actually Him and not a ghost walking on the water in the midst of the storm. Jesus called them to do the unnatural in the midst of the supernatural. Jesus called them to do everything that was against the long understood and accepted natural of everything they knew about life on earth and their world.

When Jesus said to them "It is I" He was literally saying, "I AM". I AM the great God almighty in your midst *(Exodus 3.14)*. I AM the One Who does exceedingly and abundantly above all that you can ask or imagine *(cf. Ephesians 3.20)*.

This fallen world of mankind would try to convince you that it is a natural thing to fear. It is a natural thing to be discouraged. It is a natural thing to be crushed, hurt, angered, mad—and the list goes on and on. But the fine print in the bottom line of sin's normal is "and there is not a whole lot you can do about it so just accept it"!

What God wants us to understand is that if we want to rise and walk above the unnatural of fallen humanity's world-view of the natural we have got to step out of the storm tossed boat, and then take another step, and then another step of faith in the Lord's supernatural work and word in and to our lives.

It is not normal or natural to love your enemies as well as your friends; to go two miles for someone you dislike when the normal is one mile; to pray for those who spitefully use you when it is normal to feel spiteful toward them; to forgive those who ask for no forgiveness over the offense they have hurt you so deeply with.

You do not see the supernatural work of God in and through your life when you cling to your little natural boat in a storm that God is walking on the top of while at the same time calling you to walk with Him.

The footprints of the miraculous are not found in minds and heads that embrace this fallen world's ideology of the unnatural of the supernatural and choose to walk in the mundane. The footprints of the miraculous are found in a born again heart that embraces the theology of the great "I AM", steps out in faith trusting the Lord of the supernatural, and chooses to follow Him in walking where He walks! Miracles ultimately flow from the heart and not the head.

[9] ...if you confess with your mouth the Lord Jesus and believe in your heart that God has raised Him from the dead, you will be saved.
[10] For with the heart one believes to righteousness, and with the mouth confession is made to salvation. *(Romans 10.1-10 NKJV)*

The work of God is ultimately a spiritual work that manifests itself in our physical and material world. What I have shared with you about forgiveness in this book simply will not work in its God designed fullness until we step out in faith in His Word and open our heart to God's supernatural work in our spirit and hearts.

God's ultimate work of transformation always begins in our spirit where His Holy Spirit begins flowing like a well and then a river up out of our deepest parts *(John 4.13-14, 23-24 & 7.37-39)* touching every area of our created being with His power of grace, love, and spiritual renewing.

And His work always begins in our spirit because it was spirit that God breathed into the lifeless body of man that made him a living being *(Genesis 2.7)*. When sin entered into the life and world of humanity it was his spirit that was separated and shut off to the things of God.

Thus the spirit is dead in trespasses and sins and consequently we are separated from God until we are spiritually born-again. The resurrection of life begins in our spirit and ultimately will be experienced in our physical body *(Ephesians 2.1-6 f; John 3.3-7; Romans 8.1-16)*. The heart, or the spirit, is where the issues of life spring from *(Proverb 4.23)*.

God's ways and thoughts are not our ways and thoughts. All of His promises, directives, and guidance simply will not work fully and completely without our pursuit of His work in us being done in harmony with His thoughts and ways. This is how God has designed and declared it—and nothing will ever change it!

[8] "For My thoughts are not your thoughts, Nor are your ways My ways," declares the LORD.

[9] "For *as* the heavens are higher than the earth, So are My ways higher than your ways And My thoughts than your thoughts.

[10] "For as the rain and the snow come down from heaven, And do not return there without watering the earth And making it bear and sprout, And furnishing seed to the sower and bread to the eater;

[11] So will My word be which goes forth from My mouth; It will not return to Me empty, Without accomplishing what I desire, And without succeeding *in the matter* for which I sent it. *(Isaiah 55.8-11 NASB95)*

You will never rise above and walk on and over the howling winds and battering waves while clinging to your little boat in fear, terror, and horror that arise from your hurts, disappointments, anger, doubt, unbelief, and despair.

It has been wisely observed: To have something you have never had you have to do something you have never done.

You might be thinking "But I have tried and it didn't work for me." Have you tried it <u>until</u> it did start working? Or have you tried it for a just a period of time and then stopped? Again, how much time commitment does it take? A life-time commitment!

# QUESTIONS

1.  Why do we see the unnatural condition of life as being natural?

2.  What point is the author seeking to make when he talks about being "upside down" versus being "right side up"?

3.  What is the point the author is making about the words of Jesus in John 3.3, 6-7 of "seeing" the Kingdom of God <u>now</u> as well as in the sense of seeing it when one enters into the eternal state after death?

4.  What is meant by the author saying that the work of God is ultimately a spiritual and supernatural work in our lives?

5.  Why does the work of salvation, the new birth, and the like begin in our heart, or, our spirit?

6.  Why are people in general uncomfortable or even outright opposed to a spiritual concept of the human nature?

7.  Are you readily and steadily experiencing a spiritual and supernatural work of God in your life?

# Section Seven

---

# PART 3 OF 3
# THREE OBSTACLES TO OBTAINING
# WHAT GOD HAS FOR YOU

---

## Obstacle Three

### God's Flow Through Flaws

# OUR OBSESSION WITH PERFECTION

*Therefore you are to be perfect, as your heavenly Father is perfect. (Matthew 5.48 NASB95)*

**I once read of a father who took his son duck hunting.** As they traveled to the hunting site he bragged to his son about being one of the top marksmen and hunters in the entire state. They reached their place and settled in to wait for the ducks. Finally a duck flew up and over them. The father expertly raised his gun and fired. The duck quacked and quacked as it kept on flying higher and higher into the sky. There was silence as the son, who believed that whatever his dad said or did was gospel, stared in disbelief at what had just happened. After a moment or so the father who had made such big claims told his boy: "Son, you have just witnessed a great miracle. There flies a dead duck!"

Although the writers of the Scriptures clearly indicate that there are none who achieve absolute perfection during their earthly sojourn we still find ourselves demanding it of others who we deem to be those of significance—a parent, a minister, a president, a teacher, a close friend, a counselor, and the list goes on. Even of ourselves.

The truth is that perfection is a growing process involving different stages of time, weather, seasons, and such. For example an apple in its earliest stage of growth is a tiny, hard, green ball that is very bitter (as a number of us can attest who just had to try one when we climbed up into trees as a child). And yet for that stage of its growth that apple is perfect. It is right where it is designed to be at that point in time.

As the season of time goes on the apple goes through different stages of growth in which it remains perfect for each particular point in time even though it has not reached its complete potential of perfection in the sense of a finished product. Then comes the final stage of time for the apple to reach full perfection as it becomes the right size, color, and delicious in taste.

And following this, in a manner of speaking, it departs this life in one manner or another as a fruit salad, apple pie, somebody's snack, or a bird's feast as it fulfills its assigned purpose by the Creator. Perfect for what it was designed by God to be.

However, there are things that can cause an apple to be imperfect such as blight, drought, infestation, and bugs to name a few. Most of us have heard the old saying, "All the devil's apples have worms." And most of us have experienced one or two of those apples. They were a disgusting disappointment.

There are many apples that never reach full perfection although they might have been perfect at some point in its stages of growth. We call them a bad apple. Most of us have come across some of those in our life and they were a let-down because we have known and tasted good apples before.

I realize that every comparison limps. We are not apples. There are many other factors involved in the perfection process in our lives—especially as a child of God. We have a mind. We get to make choices based on our reasoning and the weighing out of options. We are involved in an unimaginable volume of entanglements and connections with many movements of life impacting forces during our lifetime. Our life is far more complex than that of an apple.

Still there is a similar enough comparison to help us get a concept and picture of the basic development of perfection going on in our lives.

With the passing of time and seasons there is a reasonable expectation of perfection in varying degrees and sense of the word as we have put forth in our apple illustration. In our marriage and family. In our education and job skills. In our leaders and government. In our ministers and churches. In our teachers and schools.

What is acceptable at one point in time may not be acceptable at a later point in time. We do not expect of a small child what we expect of a grown adult. What is perfect for one state in time is not perfect for a later time. What is right-on at one time is way-off at another time.

For the most part we understand these things, but we can still have an unreasonable expectation of perfection, even an obsession with it in certain settings and seasons of life. Of a certain child. Our spouse. A minister. A leader. A teacher.

There are those areas where we leave little if any room for a mistake, a bad day, for losing it, betraying a confidence, failing to speak up on behalf of someone when we felt they should, and the list goes on.

Still it is a fact. We do not live in a perfect world with perfect people under perfect conditions. There are storms, droughts, blight, disease and the like not only in connection with trees, grass, and plants, but also in our ongoing life of people relationships. And imperfect conditions can produce less than a perfect life and people.

There are no perfect parents, spouses, preachers, teachers, children, siblings, friends, doctors, nurses, bosses, employees, business owners, companies, churches, homes, families, sales persons, repair persons, or anyone else anywhere else.

We are well aware of the presence of imperfections in life and people. However, we also still demand perfection of life and especially certain people to varying degrees and depths. And as a consequence we put ourselves in a position to be deeply hurt and offended by flaws and imperfections.

## THE OBSTACLE OF IMPERFECT PEOPLE

Let's come back to the storm and text setting of Matthew 14 through which God gives us some definite principles and insights for the obstacles we must overcome and rise above to obtain the fullness of life that God promises us as we pursue His heart via that small gate on the narrow way of salvation *(Matthew 7.13-14)*.

> [26] When the disciples saw Him walking on the sea, they were terrified, and said, "It is a ghost!" And they cried out in fear.
> [27] But immediately Jesus spoke to them, saying, "Take courage, it is I; do not be afraid." [28] Peter said to Him, "Lord, if it is You, command me to come to You on the water."
> [29] And He said, "Come!" And Peter got out of the boat, and walked on the water and came toward Jesus.
> [30] But seeing the wind, he became frightened, and beginning to sink, he cried out, "Lord, save me!"
> [31] Immediately Jesus stretched out His hand and took hold of him, and said to him, "You of little faith, why did you doubt?" *(Matthew 14.68-31 NASB95)*

**PETER'S SUCCESS—AND FAILURE.** When the ball, so to speak, was pitched Peter swung and connected. He had a good solid hit that sent the ball well out into the field of play. He got out of the boat at Jesus' word and he succeeded at doing what no other person outside of Jesus has ever done. He walked on the water. He walked toward Jesus. And on very stormy waters at that.

However, he was put out before reaching home plate. He took his eyes off of Jesus and began looking at the wind's natural effect all around and beneath him. While doing so he began to sink.

But two things are to be noted here. First, he did not drown. Second, he had the presence of mind to call on Jesus to save him from the fast approaching catastrophe. And yet in the midst of great success there was failure. He let fear replace his faith. He doubted and began to sink.

As long as Peter's eyes were on Jesus he walked on the water at the Lord's word. He did the unnatural of the supernatural in the midst of the natural unnatural of this present life.

When he got his eyes off of Jesus and back on the natural he ceased doing the unnatural of the supernatural. When he looked down and around instead of straight ahead he began moving in the direction he was looking—sinking in the storm winds and waves of the natural. We always move in the direction we are looking and focused on.

> We always move in the direction we are looking and focused on.

We don't have to use our imagination very much to figure out how this whole episode played out in the minds and eyes of the spectators in the boat when they saw Peter walk and then sink. You probably could hear comments like: "Well there he goes again." "He seems to get off to a fantastic start and then fizzles at the finish."

There are few things in life that deeply offend and hurt us like the imperfections in a man or woman of God whether they are a pastor, evangelist, deacon, teacher, parent, singer, musician, or a dear friend.

And there are very few of us that have lived for any appreciable length of time that have not experienced the deep disappointment of seeing someone that we believed in go through a shift of focus and begin to doubt and sink.

We struggle greatly and some of us even fall when our heroes or those we deeply admire and respect have their flaws revealed. Flaws carry a definite threat and potential of not only disappointing us, but of disillusioning and even devastating us. What can bless us greatly can also curse us greatly. What can lift us up high can also bury us equally as deep.

To Peter's credit he did get out of the dugout, swing and connect with the ball. He did walk for a time on the waters. He failed—but at least he failed trying (and for a short while doing). The other eleven fellow spectators and easy chair experts never had enough faith to get out of the dugout and consequently failed to even try.

Everyone who tries is going to both succeed and also fail on occasions. Nobody bats a 1.000. Baseball's most successful hitters, home run heroes, and those who put the runs up on the score board have a batting average well under .500. Most are probably between .300 to .390. That means for every one time they get a run they strike out around two times. One success, two failures.

But even though we know all of this we still look for that elusive absolute perfection in our church and family leaders. And even though we understand the concept of no one is perfect we still find ourselves offended, hurt, and disappointed when they are not.

We have to remind ourselves that the games that are won consist of successes and failures; of a team rather than just one or two players. That winning is succeeding enough to rise above the opponent.

## WHAT DO WE TEND TO REMEMBER THE MOST
## ABOUT PETER AND THIS STORM?

First, we remember Peter sinking. Second, we remember Peter crying out to be saved and Jesus having to rescue Peter from his embarrassing failure. Third, we remember Jesus reprimanding Peter for his lack of faith.

But few of us remember that Peter did for a brief time walk on the water.

*"And Peter got out of the boat, and walked on the water and came toward Jesus."*

And as we said previously, he was the only other man in history besides Jesus that did so.

Most all of us might have remembered Peter's success had he made it all the way to where Jesus was, getting a big bear hug from the Lord as he walked back with Jesus to the boat as the Lord laughed and congratulated him, and then getting into the boat with Jesus while receiving high fives from the other disciples.

Still there are some comforting truths here: 1) when we ask God for something and He says "yes" then we can step out in faith and He will be there to sustain us; 2) even though Peter began to sink Jesus reached out to 'un-sink' him and get him back into the boat; 3) Peter learned an invaluable lesson to keep His eyes on Jesus instead of the surrounding circumstances just as in Matthew 16 he would learn to keep his ears open to all that Jesus says; 4) God takes our sinking experiences and turns them into saving experiences; and 5) God takes our failures and uses them to make us a success.

# IMPERFECTION IMPASSE

Think with me about this. If everything we are to receive from the Lord has to come through perfect ministers, parents, teachers, and other significant people then we will not be receiving much of anything from God any time soon in this present time.

Peter went on to have a powerful apostolic ministry that would see countless thousands come into the kingdom of God, many people healed, and churches established. Did he become a perfect minister without any further flaws appearing in his life? No.

But think about Peter's life and ministry from the start to our last word about him in Scriptures. Earlier Peter in his great confession of Jesus as the Christ, the Son of the living God, a few moments later contradicted the statements of Christ on His impending crucifixion and resurrection *(Matthew 16.15-23)*. He had part of the picture right and part of it wrong. But the wrong did not cancel out what was right. In fact, the right perception would soon correct the wrong perception.

Peter cut off the ear of Malcus, the servant of the High Priest, when they came to take Jesus captive on the crucifixion eve *(John 18.10-11 cf. Luke 22.51)*. Did that impulsive act (that Jesus corrected by miraculously restoring the ear) nullify the healings that Peter did as one of the twelve sent out before Christ was crucified and would later occur under Peter's apostolic ministry after Jesus' resurrection? No.

Peter would be the one chosen by God to be the first to open the doors of the kingdom of God to the Gentiles *(Acts 10-11)*, but later be reproved by Paul for displaying prejudice against the Gentiles *(Galatians 2.11-14)*. Did this slip up of a character flaw involving prejudice coming from years of his Jewish upbringing nullify what God did for the Gentiles under his ministry? No.

Peter became an apostle and minister greatly used of God. He would preach the church's first sermon on the day of Pentecost declaring Jesus' crucifixion, death, resurrection, ascension back to heaven, and sending the outpouring of the Holy Spirit. He declared clearly Who Jesus is and what He is doing and it resulted in seeing over 3,000 turn to Christ *(Acts 2)*.

He and John would be instrumental in the healing of the lame man at the Gate Beautiful *(Acts 3)*. It is implied that people would be healed when Peter's shadow fell across them on the streets of Jerusalem *(Acts 5.15)*. He would later author two books of the New Testament bearing his name. The list goes on.

Peter was part of the inner circle of three that Jesus took with Him when raising Jarius' daughter from the dead, when going up to be transfigured on the mountain, and when going into Gethsemane's garden to pray for strength when facing the coming crucifixion.

Still, Peter had definite flaws that manifested themselves over a course of many years of discipleship and ministry. John along with his brother James, the other two members of the inner circle, also had flaws. They wanted to call fire down from heaven to consume a Samaritan village when they were offended by people the Jews held very deep prejudice and disdain for *(Luke 9.54)*.

The apostle Paul and Barnabas had a very heated disagreement over the future ministry of John Mark (the same Mark who would later write the Gospel bearing his name). Because of Mark's failure during their first missionary journey Paul rejected Mark from traveling with them a second time (as in a second chance).

The renowned evangelistic team separated from one another over this very sharp dispute *(Acts 15.36-40)* which no doubt was seen by many as flaws in the highest realm of church leadership. Paul would later write in a letter to Timothy, the young man many believe Paul used to replace Mark, that *"Mark... is useful to me in ministry" (II Timothy 4.11)* indicating that Barnabas had been right about a second chance.

Did this contentious difference of opinion between two great men of God and their sharp separation from one another in ministry change the many, many wonderful things that God had done through their years together—and would continue to do through them individually? No.

In the Old Testament, Abraham, the father of faith, out of fear for his life told a half-lie about Sarah as being his sister rather than his wife. Sarah wound up being taken as a wife for another man and only God's intervention saved the couple from a great disaster. Yet this does not nullify that God used them and today we are blessed because of them.

David, declared to be a man after God's own heart, committed adultery with a woman named Bathsheba who was married to one of David's top thirty soldier heroes and she conceived a child in this act of adultery. He then occasioned the death of her husband by manipulation in a theater of war to cover his indiscretion and sin. These were not just unseemly personality or character flaws—they were great sins. He would fail to properly discipline and guide several of his children (very likely due to his own example of moral failure) and they in turn would later cause him deep grief and heart break. Later David in pride numbered his army in disobedience to God's Word.

But does David's flaws and failures nullify the truths of his many Psalms such as Psalm 23, 27, 34, 36 and 103 to name just a few? Do we reject God's flow of revelation and truth through a flawed man or do we receive it in spite of flaws while understanding the struggle of flaws inherent in human nature while not inanely excusing them?

## GOD'S FLOW THROUGH FLAWS

Again, there are no perfect or flawless ministers, teachers, parents, leaders, singers, and others we could name. If God did not use flawed people then there would be no one for God to use on planet earth to fill, flow through, and minister to us. There is no one good enough to raise children. There is no one perfect enough to lead us. There is no one of unflawed character for God to flow through in songs. There is no one to be our friend. For all of us are flawed.

Thank God, because we are flawed does not mean we have to keep making the same mistakes over and over or excusing them. This does not mean that we keep committing the same sins over and over. But it does mean there will be mistakes and wrongs that happen. Even sin. This means that we will always need to lean on the grace and wisdom of God. This means that fish will still come with bones and that we will still have to be willing to spit the bones out if we want to receive the nutrition that comes from eating the fish.

I believe you understand by what I have said throughout this book that God does not excuse nor expect us to keep committing the same wrongs and offenses over and over without overcoming them. When there is conviction of sin and wrong, a genuine turning to the Lord, and a putting away the sin and its failures God responds by cleansing, restoring, and empowering us to overcome (e.g., Psalm 51).

My wife has been used of the Lord to develop and lead some small and large women's ministries (running in the hundreds) both in our local church groups as well as in interdenominational circles. She invited a woman to come as a speaker who was just beginning to rise in public awareness as an effective minister to women. The speaker brushed my wife off by indicating to her the particular group at that time was not large enough for her ministry. This did not create a great admiration and appreciation for this woman nor her ministry for either my wife or me. But this woman went on to have a very large national ministry and God has flowed through her various teachings that have blessed literally tens upon tens of thousands—including my wife and myself.

God raised up a man who had a powerful ministry on prayer that was greatly used of the Lord for several years. His ministry and teachings were instrumental in developing a much stronger and enlarged prayer life in me. I in turn used his timely and insightful teachings to lead our own congregations into enlarged and intense prayer lives. Then came a time when this man fell into greed and pride. His home, his reputation, and his ministry were wrecked because of it. But did this nullify and cancel out the truths that he brought to the church during his faithful and committed years? Were his teachings and truths to be thrown out because he was flawed. No! God's truth is not flawed although the teacher may be. Again, you thank God for the fish He provides, then you eat the fish He gives, and spit out the bones God has hung the meat on.

Truth is truth whether it comes through a mighty prophet or through a prophet's donkey that has more spirituality than the prophet.

It was a young man in high school that was directly instrumental in my senior year of my coming to the Lord. He was a young man with numerous flaws. He said things that were truth but his conduct was for the most part not in harmony with that truth. The words he spoke about the Lord and church were truth. The works of his day to day living were flawed.

But I attended church through his invitation. I was saved as a result and have been following the Lord as a Christian for over fifty-eight years at the writing of this book and as a minister for over fifty-six years. The Lord has blessed me with a precious wife with whom I just celebrated 55 years of marriage in June of 2013. Both of my brothers came to the Lord and are ministers. Two of my three sons are in the ministry (one in music and the other in youth). I presently have nine grand-children and five great-grandchildren who are in church. Two at this point have indicated feeling a call to the ministry.

I am so thankful that I received God's flow through flaws to my life. I thank God for the fish and bread in his miraculous feeding to my life and the good sense to spit out the bones. I thank God that truth is truth and that His Word never returns to Him without accomplishing that for which He sends it.

Thank God that even though His flow to us comes through imperfect people to imperfect people that His flow of grace and love is pure and perfect bringing us to the position of perfect standing in a perfect Savior—Jesus Christ our Lord.

You must reach out and embrace God's flow coming through flaws. God gives us His treasures in earthen vessels *(II Corinthians 4.7)*. It is not the vessel—it is the treasure that enriches.

Thank God for the many, many countless men and women that have pursued and become vessels of gold, silver, and honor *(II Timothy 2.20-21)*. They in themselves become a treasure of great loveliness to our lives as well.

But, there are still a lot of cracked pots and plates along with paper throw-a-ways that have contained some delicious meals. We receive the good that God sends through those vessels but we don't keep these vessels in our china closet.

We must learn the secret of facing the fact of flaws rather than fleeing from flaws. We must reject the wrong of flaws while receiving the flow of God coming through those flaws. We must not let our fear of flaws stop our faith in God's faithful flow through flaws to our lives.

And remember, God's flow through flaws is coming to those with flaws to help us overcome those very or similar flaws in our lives. Don't let the sword of a fleshly zealot stop you from rejoicing over the healing of a severed ear. Don't allow the sinking of a fearful disciple to distract you from the faith of that same disciple to walk in the power of the unnatural of the supernatural in the midst of the natural.

The same disciple that started sinking in the storm that night would rise in God's grace and power to become a mighty apostle that would weather victoriously many storms in the future and become one of the reasons we know the Lord today. God took this weak flawed reed and turned him into a mighty rock of ministry for the kingdom *(John 1.42; Luke 22.31-32)*.

I have a plaque that says: "So it is not home sweet home—adjust!" Remember, this present earth is not heaven. It is one of the reasons we look forward to the new heaven, the new earth, and the New Jerusalem where all that offends is removed and we will receive God's flow in a flawless world.

But until then we live as a flawed people in a flawed world that must in faith take God's flow through flaws from the flawless Christ to grow in His ongoing work of perfection in our lives and receive all the fullness of the abundant life in Christ He has for us.

When a person is lost or stranded on a dessert or in the wilderness it is not wise nor does it pay to get fussy about who brings you water. If you wait for perfect people to bring you water you will never live to get a drink.

When Jesus and Peter, the Flawless One and the flawed one, got into the boat, the disciples did not dwell on their flawed brother in the faith. They all together worshipped the Christ Who is the great I AM.

[32] When they got into the boat, the wind stopped.
[33] And those who were in the boat worshiped Him, saying, "You are certainly God's Son!" *(Matthew 14.32-33 NASB95)*

To obtain all that God has for us in His plans and provisions for our lives we must overcome these Three Obstacles to Obtaining. We must overcome the grind of time, the unnatural of the supernatural, and God's flow through flaws to obtain the full flow of life God is sending through Christ to our lives.

# THOUGHTS

## The Blend and Balance of God's Supernatural Work in this Natural World and Our Lives

[34] When they had crossed over, they came to land at Gennesaret.
[35] And when the men of that place recognized Him, they sent *word* into all that surrounding district and brought to Him all who were sick;
[36] and they implored Him that they might just touch the fringe of His cloak; and as many as touched *it* were cured. *(Matthew 14.34-36 NASB95)*

It is worth noting that Jesus is the One Who urged and made the disciples get into that particular boat in Matthew 14 to go to the other side of the sea while He remained on the shore.

Did Jesus know about the coming storm? If so, why did He have His disciples leave at that particular time? Why not wait until the storm had come and gone?

Whatever the circumstances and reasons for our Lord's choosing this time, place, and boat all of the disciples finished the journey in the very same boat that Jesus had started them out in.

Both the storm and Jesus' walking on the water were an interlude in a God ordained journey made in a boat chosen by Him across the sea from one place of supernatural ministry (the feeding of the 5,000 men) to another place of supernatural ministry to yet another host of people in need.

We live in a world created by God that operates under the laws of nature designed by God. Though God can and on occasions has suspended those physical laws of the natural and worked in human existence by laws of the supernatural it is not often or for long.

And even when God intervenes, such as he did in another storm many years later that was about to take the life of the apostle Paul and the other 275 aboard a ship, the Lord still balances the use of the natural and the supernatural *(Acts 27)*. God promised Paul in a supernatural visit by an angel that although the ship would be lost all 276 lives on board would be saved.

When the ship came to shallower water and the sailors sensed land nearby they planned to sneak off in a smaller boat and save their own lives. Paul declared to the Roman centurion that if the sailors left them there would be a loss of the remaining lives. So the smaller boat the sailors were planning on using to make their escape was cut loose and all remained aboard, including the skilled sailors.

Although God could have done it all supernaturally he chose to use the skill of the sailors to get all of them as close to shore as possible. When the ship got as close as it could it became stuck in the sand where the waters were turbulent and moving in very strong cross currents. The ship broke apart but all were able to either swim or take pieces of the broken boat and make it to the safety of the shore and thus all 276 were saved as Paul had been told by God's angel and had boldly declared to the crew and passengers.

Come back to the Matthew 14 storm. The disciples were caught in this storm because at the Lord's command they obediently got into a particular boat going to a particular place at a particular time.

As a result of their obedience the storm that came occasioned a further revelation of the divinity and power of Jesus resulting in them worshiping Him. Together they reached the Gennesaret shores where further works of the supernatural were experienced.

Again, the point is this: they started the journey in the boat chosen by the Lord at a time chosen by the Him and they finished that divine journey of both supernatural and natural events in that same boat together.

We don't always understand all the ways the Lord chooses to work but this we can understand—the opportunities for these particular divinely ordained times of God's supernatural manifestations came at that particular appointed time in that particular appointed boat and at no other time and in no other boat.

Don't try to figure God out. Don't let the times God chooses either in point or length become an obstacle to obtaining. Don't let the unnatural of the supernatural become an obstacle to obtaining. And don't let God's flow through flaws become an obstacle to obtaining.

Let God use the time He has created for His ordained purposes in your life and go the distance. Let God work in your life in supernatural power and working to do the unnatural in the midst of the natural. And let God's flow through flaws fill your heart and life by receiving and flowing with and in that life-flow from God. That flow from God will carry you to the shores of His abundant life.

**Only God and God Alone is Perfect, Good, and Flawless!**

One of the saddest mistakes we can make in life is expecting someone else to be what only God can be to our lives. Your spouse can never be nor do for you what only God can do. Your parents can never be what only God can be. Your best friend can never be what only God can be. Your children can never be what only God can be. No doubt there are others you can add to this list.

We must be careful what we expect and demand of people in our lives. When we go beyond the humanly possible and reasonable we set both ourselves and the vital relationships we need and have with others on a course of failure and disappointment. Nobody can be to us what only God can be. All the rest of us get tired, exhausted, impatient, mouthy, overly demanding, lacking in total 24/7 appreciation, short on gifts and ability, distracted, and the like to be every moment, every hour, of every day of every week what the other person needs.

We all have to have our space and down time. We do not have endless resources of strength, supplies, and support to give to each other. All of us come to the end of ourselves because we are finite and limited.

Only God is omniscient, omnipotent, and omnipresent. The rest of us know in part and see through a glass darkly; run out of gas; and, are just not always able to be there when we need to be.

What we have to offer each other can be good, uplifting, and sufficient on occasions, even many occasions—but not all the time and every time.

To expect a significant other to be what only God can be is doomed to failure by its very definition of our expectations—and even smacks of idol worship.

Rejoice in the one and ones that God gives to your life. Love them for who they are—someone a lot like you. Stay in fellow-ship (i.e., fellow travelers in the same ship rowing for the same shore).

Let God be God and all others be the best they can in your life. But never forget that your ultimate identification and well being has always and will always rest in the hand of none other or less than God Himself. He is the only One fully capable of flawless support of our lives and well being.

# QUESTIONS

1.  Why do we have such high expectations of perfection in people who we admire or who are significant to our lives?

2.  What does the apple illustration show you about perfection?

3.  What do you think the author means by "every comparison limps"?

4.  What flaws can you think of that people may have that are not necessarily sinful in themselves but still offend and are a turn off to you?

5.  What flaws do you think someone can have and still be acceptable enough for God to use them?

6.  Can you think of other Biblical characters that the author did not mention that God used in spite of their flaws? For example, Samson. What others?

7.  Can you think of any well known ministries or ministers with flaws that God has used—and some He may still be using?

8.  Are there flaws that you feel are unacceptable or even unforgiveable in nature? What and why are they unacceptable.

9.  Have you ever experienced the deep hurt of a flaw manifested in someone you greatly admired? How did you handle it? Did that flaw negate for you all the good things that person had brought to your life?

10. What does the concept of God's Flow Through Flaws say to you? Perhaps it would be good to make a list of all the truths that The Three Obstacles to Obtaining have spoken to your hear—or further questions that they may have raised in your mind.

11. In Thoughts what do the author's points about the blend of the natural and the supernatural say to you personally about God's working in your life?

# KEEP ON KEEPING ON

"And do not be conformed to this world, but be transformed by the renewing of your mind, that you may prove what is that good and acceptable and perfect will of God." *(ROMANS 12.2 NKJV)*

It is very important that you understand that for all of your life, up to the time that you surrendered your heart to Christ as your Lord and were saved (born-again), that your mind has been trained to think and respond to offenses in a world-view that does not include what is right in the sight of the Lord as revealed in the Word of God.

Overwhelmingly, your teachers and sources of information were not the Lord nor His Word but those whose minds were not renewed and serving the Lord (except, of course, for the times we were in places and on the occasions where God's Word was being taught).

As a consequence you bring other baggage and ideas into your walk with the Lord that are not always from Him. The longer you lived before the time you surrendered your life to Christ the more baggage and ideas you have in your thinking to deal with. This is one reason that the older a person becomes the less likely they are to come to Christ as their Savior if they have not done so earlier in life.

It is clear from the Word of God that a new way of thinking and responding must flow from your mind, based on the Scriptures, that results in God's transforming power working in your life through the power of the Holy Spirit dwelling now in you.

You will not find it an easy thing to change from a life of habits and a mind-set developed over the years that have become a *"weight"* and *"the sin which so easily ensnares"* (See Hebrews 12.1). The satanic and demonic does not want you to change. The sinful flesh-nature does not want you to change.

I have shared a considerable volume of information with you about forgiveness in this book so it may be necessary from time to time to review the truths.

There will, undoubtedly, be times when the old flesh feelings of hate, revenge, and the like will try to regain dominance in your life—especially when new and fresh offenses arise.

However, the effort and constant vigilance of your heart against unforgiveness and seeking to deal with offenses through forgiveness will be more than worth the effort and time required.

A very popular maxim that I heard frequently after I came to the Lord was: "You have to keep on keeping on."

Our blessing and hope that we now have is found in the victories and advances made by doing it God's way.

The more and longer you do it God's way, the deeper and stronger the commitment will be in your life, that is reinforced by that peace that passes all understanding *(Philippians 4.7)* and by His joy that is unspeakable *(I Peter 1.8)*.

I asked early in this book: "How much faith do you have to have to see God's Word work in your life?" And the answer is: "Just enough to embrace His promises and instructions for your life, and to step out and do what He tells you to do."

In faith, keep on keeping on!

# APPENDIX

# TASTE AND SEE

**PSALM 34.8** *(NKJV)* **Oh, taste and see that the LORD *is* good; Blessed *is* the man who trusts in Him!**

**PSALM 119.103** *(NKJV)* **How sweet are Your words to my taste, *Sweeter* than honey to my mouth!**

Is the Bible and the ideas of the Christian faith new to you? If so, God invites you to take a TASTE-TEST. He invites you to give it a try. You are invited to step out, take God at His Word, and see what will happen in your life.

For most of us who have been serving the Lord for many years this is how it started. It did for me. I was raised in one church group. I took instructions in another church group and was just one step from confirmation when I accepted an invitation from people of yet another church group to attend some services. I heard the Bible, the Word of God, preached in the service I attended. Something began stirring inside of me.

I went home and found a copy of the New Testament of the Bible. I began reading in the Gospel of Matthew. I continued reading for about three weeks. As I did so that stirring grew stronger and stronger. I was tasting. I then began to see. In a short time I found that truly *"the LORD is good"* and that *"blessed is the man who trusts in Him!"*

## DRINK AND LIVE

**JOHN 4.13-14** *(NKJV)* **Jesus...said..., "Whoever drinks...of the water that I shall give him will never thirst. But the water that I shall give him will become in him a fountain of water springing up into everlasting life."**

**JOHN 7.37–39** *(NKJV)* [37] **...Jesus stood and cried out, saying, "If any one thirsts, let him come to Me and drink.** [38] **He who believes in Me, as the Scripture has said, out of his heart will flow rivers of living water."** [39] **But this He spoke concerning the Spirit, whom those believing in Him would receive...**

Once you have tasted and then you begin to drink from God's fountain of living water (His Word, Presence, Power) you experience life on a quality level that you never dreamed was possible. Life that is eternal fills and transforms your old way of living. Now you have moved beyond tasting to drinking. He has given you a *"fountain of water springing up into everlasting life"*.

Now you know that God is not only good but He is the very essence of eternal life that is filling you.

# FEED AND GROW

JOHN 6.34...63 *(NKJV)* [35] And Jesus said to them, "I am the bread of life. He who comes to Me shall never hunger, and he who believes in Me shall never thirst. [47] Most assuredly, I say to you, he who believes in Me has everlasting life. [48] I am the bread of life. [51] I am the living bread which came down from heaven. If anyone eats of this bread, he will live forever; and the bread that I shall give is My flesh, which I shall give for the life of the world. [63] It is the Spirit who gives life; ...The words that I speak to you are spirit, and *they* are life."

At the time I am writing these words to you I have been serving the Lord for 58 years. Out of those years I have been in ministry 56 years. There have been many ups and downs, ins and outs, but in all of it I have come to see how faithful God is to His Word and work in my life. I now know that He *"is able to do exceedingly abundantly above all that we ask or think, according to the power that works in us"* (Ephesians 3:20 NKJV)

And I have met literally thousands of men and women who serve the Lord and one thing marks them all. The longer they have walked with the Lord the more they have found that He is faithful to do all that He has promised to do.

So, dear reader, if you haven't TASTED yet why not start now. You too will find that the LORD is good, and blessed are all that put their trust in Him. LET GO AND LET GOD WORK!

I invite you to do these 6 simple things:

1. **Take a step of faith.** Bow your head and as you turn from sin and wrong doing ask God, in the name of Jesus Christ, to forgive you for all your sins and wrong doing and to give you strength to live right.

2. **Ask Jesus to come into your life as your Lord and Savior** and to give you a heart to serve Him. Surrender your heart and life to Him. Repent (turn from sin) and let Him be your Lord.

3. **Begin reading the Word of God (the Bible) regularly.** I suggest starting in the New Testament with the Gospel of Matthew *(for now read*

*lightly over the long list of family names in verses 1-17 and start your focused reading with verse 18).* After Matthew I suggest the following order: The Gospel of John; I John; Ephesians; Colossians; The Gospel of Luke; The Book of Acts; then Mark and Romans on through the remaining NT books you have not read. Read at least two or so chapters a day.

4. **Read one Psalm and some from Proverbs each day** as well (found in the Old Testament). **Pray and praise the Lord** *(see Matthew 6.9-13 for Jesus' powerful prayer blueprint for your prayer life).*

5. **Begin each Scripture reading for the day with asking God to open His Word to your understanding for your life.** Some of what you read will be understood and begin working quickly; the other will be understood and work in your life in the coming days, weeks, months, and years.

6. **Find, attend, and become a part of a good Bible believing, preaching, and teaching church.** As you are faithful in reading the Bible also pray for the Lord to lead you in finding a good church home. He will guide you and you will sense which one should be your church home.

How much faith do you have to have to see God's Word work in your life? All you need is enough to embrace His promises for your life—and to step out and do what He tells you to do a step at a time.

Jesus made a promise to everyone that when you pursue God in prayer and earnestly reach out to Him that He will respond and answer. Read Jesus' promise for yourself:

MATTHEW 7:7–11 *(NKJV)* ⁷ **"ASK, and it will be given to you; SEEK, and you will find; KNOCK, and it will be opened to you.**

⁸ **"For <u>EVERYONE</u> who ASKS receives, and he who SEEKS finds, and to him who KNOCKS it will be opened.**

⁹ **"Or what man is there among you who, if his son asks for bread, will give him a stone?**

¹⁰ **"Or if he asks for a fish, will he give him a serpent?**

¹¹ **"If you then, being evil, know how to give good gifts to your children, HOW MUCH MORE WILL YOUR FATHER WHO IS IN HEAVEN GIVE GOOD THINGS TO THOSE WHO ASK HIM!"** *(words in all caps I have done for emphasis).*

The ask, seek, and knock sequence in the English language of the word ASK makes a good acrostic.

# <u>A</u> = Ask   <u>S</u> = Seek   <u>K</u> = Knock

There are many excellent translations of the Bible into English to start your journey of discovery with. I would suggest starting with either the **New King James Version** or the **New International Version**.

**"Blessed are those who hear the word of God and keep it!"**
**(Luke 11.28 NKJV)**

# WHAT IS THE BIBLE?

**The word "bible" itself basically means "book".** When we speak of the Holy Bible we are speaking of a book that is regarded as holy and sacred coming to us ultimately from God Himself.

There is a reason the Bible has become the most circulated and sought after book throughout its history in mankind's existence. IT WORKS! No other book has come close to having the enduring impact upon human history like the Bible in shaping nations, cultures, literature, art, philosophy, education, morals, and through the transformation of the lives of men and women, youth and children. No other book has brought such great spiritual awakenings.

Wherever the Bible has gone whether in print, in spoken word, electronic forms, and the like—lives, thinking, and behavior have been radically changed. Lives in bondage have been set free, broken hearts have been mended, hope has become a reality, and vibrant faith blossoms. Men and women have been willing to literally lay down their lives in death or spend their lives in service by sending forth the Bible's message of God's love in salvation to others.

Countless millions upon millions of people through the ages have found God's promises contained in the Bible literally fulfilled in their lives. I am one of those people, for which I deeply thank our Lord Jesus Christ.

And I am so appreciative of the continuing chain of faithful men and women who have passed this priceless treasure on from generation to generation long before America was a nation—many at a great cost to their own lives.

Here is a glimpse of just a few of the many powerful, beautiful declarations, and promises from the Bible that are for you as they are, will be, and have been for all men and women through the ages that hear and embrace them. I will put in all capital lettering for emphasis that which has to do with the Word of God and add some brackets *| | expanding the key thought.

**HEBREWS 4.12** *(NKJV)* **For THE WORD OF GOD is living and powerful, and sharper than any two-edged sword, piercing even to the division of soul and spirit, and of joints and marrow, and is a discerner of the thoughts and intents of the heart.**

**I PETER 1.23–25** *(NKJV)* **[23] having been born again, not of corruptible seed but incorruptible, through THE WORD OF GOD which lives and abides forever, [24] because 'All flesh is as grass, and all the glory of man as the flower of the grass. The grass withers, and its flower falls away, [25] but THE WORD OF THE LORD endures forever.' Now this is THE WORD which by the gospel was preached to you."**

**II TIMOTHY 3.16–17** *(NKJV)* [16] All SCRIPTURE is given by inspiration* of God, and is profitable for doctrine, for reproof, for correction, for instruction in righteousness, [17] that the man of God may be complete, thoroughly equipped for every good work. *[i.e., God breathed]*

**ISAIAH 55.10–11** *(NKJV)* [10] For as the rain comes down, and the snow from heaven, and do not return there, but water the earth, and make it bring forth and bud, that it may give seed to the sower and bread to the eater, [11] So shall MY WORD be that goes forth from My mouth; IT shall not return to Me void*, but IT shall accomplish what I please, and IT shall prosper** in the thing for which I sent IT. *[i.e., empty, without results]  **[succeed, achieve]*

**II PETER 1.3–4** *(NKJV)* [3] His divine power has given to us all things that pertain to life and godliness, through the knowledge of Him who called us by glory and virtue, [4] by which have been given to us EXCEEDINGLY GREAT AND PRECIOUS PROMISES*, that through THESE you may be partakers of the divine nature, having escaped the corruption in the world through lust. *[this is His Word!]*

**PSALM 1.1–3** *(NKJV)* [1] Blessed is the man Who walks not in the counsel of the ungodly, Nor stands in the path of sinners, Nor sits in the seat of the scornful; [2] But his delight is in THE LAW OF THE LORD, And in HIS LAW he meditates day and night. [3] He shall be like a tree planted by the rivers of water, That brings forth its fruit in its season, Whose leaf also shall not wither; And whatever he does shall prosper.

**John 15.4–7** *(NKJV)* JESUS SAID: [4] "Abide in Me, and I in you. As the branch cannot bear fruit of itself, unless it abides in the vine, neither can you, unless you abide in Me. [5] I am the vine, you are the branches. He who abides in Me, and I in him, bears much fruit; for without Me you can do nothing. [6] If anyone does not abide in Me, he is cast out as a branch and is withered; and they gather them and throw them into the fire, and they are burned. [7] If you abide in Me, and MY WORDS abide in you, you will ask what you desire, and it shall be done for you."

**JOHN 8.31–32** *(NKJV)* [31] Then Jesus said to those Jews who believed Him, "If you abide in MY WORD, you are My disciples indeed. [32] And you shall know THE TRUTH, and THE TRUTH shall make you free."

**JOSHUA 1.8** *(NKJV)* This BOOK OF THE LAW shall not depart from your mouth, but you shall meditate in IT day and night, that you may observe to do according to all that is WRITTEN IN it. For then you will make your way prosperous, and then you will have good success.

<u>ROMANS 10.8–10, 13, 17</u> *(NKJV)* [8] But what does it say? "THE WORD is near you, even in your mouth and in your heart" (that is, THE WORD OF FAITH which we preach): [9] that if you confess with your mouth the Lord Jesus and believe in your heart that God has raised Him from the dead, you will be saved. [10] For with the heart one believes to righteousness, and with the mouth confession is made to salvation. [13] For "whoever calls upon the name of the Lord shall be saved." [17] So then faith comes by hearing, and hearing by THE WORD OF GOD.

There are many others. You can discover the joy of reading them in the Bible for yourself.

Just know this, God's Word will work for and in you as it has for countless multitudes upon multitudes *[literally, millions]* of others in all nations and cultures through the centuries of the world where the Word of God, the Holy Bible, has come.

You do not have to be an exception. Start by praying right now that God will come to you in His love and grace as you open your heart to His salvation in His Son, Jesus Christ. You will be surprisingly amazed to see what God is going to do in your life as you set your heart to follow Him through reading, listening, and DOING what the Word of God tells you to do.

"Heaven and earth will pass away, but MY WORDS will by no means pass away." *Jesus in Mark 13:31 (NKJV)*

# WHAT IS THE CHURCH?

**There are many who find themselves confused over exactly what the church is and which one of the many, if any, is really the right or true one.** The subject of Ecclesiology (study and doctrine of the Church) is among one of the most important doctrines in the Christian faith and in God's plan for the human race. Here I will share just some very basic and brief observations for you to consider.

I am also including on the page following this article my simple visual aid with symbols to illustrate this great truth in a way that I think will help you get a grasp on what the Church is.

The word and concept of "church" in the Greek *(the language of the New Testament and the Septuagint translation of the Old Testament)*, including the general Bible usage before the New Testament, basically means "an assembly" or "an assembly of called out ones". Other words for church that could be used are assembly, congregation, or gathering.

In the New Testament, after the death, resurrection, ascension of Christ back to heaven, and the outpouring of the Holy Spirit, the word "church" is used overwhelmingly in reference of and to all who put their trust and faith in Jesus Christ as their Lord and Savior thus experiencing regeneration (salvation, conversion, born-again, new birth). These now make up the past, present, and future Church.

There are many historical branches of the Church and Christianity with various names that serve to identify them in their historical and doctrinal settings. And yet there is only one true Church.

In what is referred to as Orthodox Christianity, which makes up the overwhelming majority of all Christendom, regardless of their church group name, approximately 95% of all stated doctrinal belief is held in common. This in itself is most remarkable. The approximate 5% variance has to do mostly with church government, certain doctrinal emphasis, or historical peculiarities.

Just as the human body, that is used to illustrate the church in I Corinthians 12, has organs and functions that vastly differ from one another but all of them together make up the human body, so it is of the one, true church. There is one Church made up of many groups.

Yes, there are unorthodox and cultic groups. Without exception what ultimately marks them from Orthodox Christianity is their doctrine (beliefs) of who Jesus is *(cf. Jesus' question' to His disciples, "Who do men say that I, the Son of Man, am?" Matthew 16.13–16)*. Remember, the only money, art, and the like that are copied, or counterfeited, are the genuine article. Without the genuine article there can be no copies or counterfeits. And consider that cancer is a real cell in the body that has become perverted and turned radical so that it no longer serves its originally designed life-giving function in the human body.

In the New Testament the one Church is first stated by Jesus in Matthew 16.13–18, clearly set forth in the Book of Acts, succinctly illustrated in I Corinthians 12 as the Body of Christ, revealed in Ephesians 1–3 to have been in the heart of God from eternity past, doctrinally defined in the epistles, and triumphantly seen in the Book of Revelation. The closer a church movement comes to that of the Book of Acts and the Epistles of the New Testament the closer it is to the very heart beat of Christ in His Church.

The one true Church is made up of individual people from the many historical branches of church groups all of whom have placed their faith in Jesus Christ as their Lord and Savior resulting in them being Born-Again as clearly taught by Jesus in John 3.

As I stated earlier, I have developed a simple visual aid of symbols to illustrate the relationship of the many different church groups to the one true Church. I have used this illustration for years in our pastorates and special services.

I use as a symbol for the one true Church a **large bold circle** with a **triangle** in the center speaking of the Triune Godhead; a **Bible** speaking of God's written Word of revelation to us; a **cross** speaking of Jesus' complete and finished work of salvation for us when He was crucified, buried, raised from the dead, and ascended back to heaven to be seated at the right hand of God the Father; and the **flying dove**, speaking of the sending forth of God's Holy Spirit to do the absolute essential spiritual work of regeneration, renewing, and imparting God's light of truth in our hearts and lives.

There are **twelve smaller circles** around the perimeter of the large bold circle (twelve being the Biblical number of divine calling) that represent all the various historical church groups and movements that have arisen through the years since the death and resurrection of Christ.

One of the twelve represents your church group if you attend a church or identify with a church group. The other circles represent the numerous other church groups (Mark 9.38–41; John 10.15-16). To the degree that those circles with the lined area intersect with the larger circle speaks of those in the various church groups who have been regenerated or born-again and thus truly have come to know Christ as their personal Lord and Savior. The closer a church group comes to the model church of Acts and the Epistles the more its circle intersects within the large center circle of the one true Church.

**In each of the outer perimeter of the circles** there is an area with no lines which contain an **encircled upside down broken cross** in them. I use this symbol because it is a symbol used by many representing either a religious or anti-religious opposition to Christ and His death on the cross for our sins—representing a pursuit of peace without the Prince of Peace. This speaks of church goers or people who profess to believe in God but reject His Church and who have not experienced Christ in their hearts and may have no desire or intention of doing so *(Luke 8.4–18; 13.23–30)*.

Also in this area of the outer perimeter circles there are **shaded areas** of varying intensity that speak of areas of that church group that have been influenced and shaped by worldly influence, secular thinking, becoming politically correct versus Biblically correct, and/or have cultic-type or other satanic/demonic doctrinal influences *(I Timothy 4.1–2 f.; II Timothy 3.1–5)*.

**Along the bold line of the large circle that intersects with the smaller ones** is where born-again Christians become influenced by the secular or cultic-type thinking and behavior and as a result live carnal lives that are more like the world than Christ a great deal of the time or in certain areas of a mind set *(I Corinthians 2.6–3.15)*.

I trust that this simple illustration will help you to comprehend some of the general basics of what the One True Church is in relationship to the many historical church groups, movements, denominations, and the like that have arisen through the years.

# THE CHURCH
## ONE VS. MANY

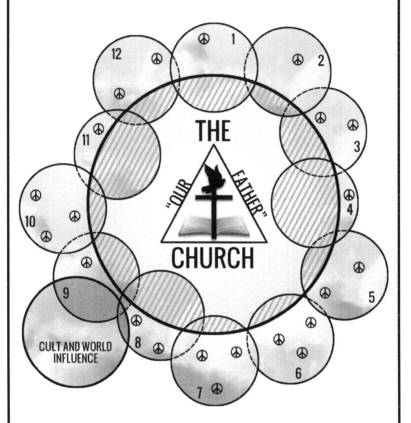

**12 Circles** The Biblical number that speaks of God's calling

&#9855; The unconverted church-goer

///// Those in various church groups who have been born again (saved, regenerated, etc.) and make up the one, true church

# THE BACKGROUND OF SOME BIBLICAL WORDS & PHRASES USED IN THIS BOOK

### GENERATION: THE ORIGINAL CREATION STATE

God created man in His image. He made mankind male and female. God formed the body of man from the dust or the very elements of the ground. Then God breathed into that lifeless body life through His Spirit. Man became a living physical / soulical / spiritual being. In God's creation of man he was made a living being comprised of a body, soul, and spirit. This is recorded in Genesis 1.26–2.25, the first book of the Bible in the Old Testament.

Through his body man has physical/material awareness; through his spirit he has spiritual awareness; and, through his soul he has self-awareness. These three intertwine tightly together so that it can be difficult to draw clear cut lines between the three—especially the soul and the spirit, the brain (physical) and mind (soul/spirit), and the like *(e.g., Hebrews 4.12; Matthew 26.41; Mark 12.30)*.

For an unspecified period of time after creation man had unbroken communion with God as he experienced physical/material awareness of the earth God had created and placed him in; experienced the inner mental and self-awareness of the life God had made him; and, experienced spiritual-awareness of God's existence and all He had created that is not seen by the physical eye.

### DE-GENERATION: THE FALLEN AND SINFUL STATE

Genesis 3.1–24 records what is referred to by students of the Scriptures as The Fall of man into sin by disobeying God's Word spoken to him. In so doing man was separated by this sin of disobedince from God and death set in. The spirit was dead in sin in the sense of being separated from God. Physical disease, dying, and death entered into our world separating man from continuing health, living, and life. Mankind morally became overall and overwhelmingly corrupt and violent with rare exception *(Genesis 4–6)*.

This affected mankind in such a way that some of the following words and phrases have become used in describing certain aspects of human behavior and mind-sets.

**THE SINFUL FLESH-NATURE; the CARNAL or CARNAL-NATURE; and the NATURAL MAN.** Broadly put these terminologies refer to that part of our human nature that has at its roots a world-view that is right in its own sight, thus sinful, versus that which is right in the sight of the Lord. This condition is also referred to as the **Adamic-Nature** due to the human nature being marred by sin in Adam when he chose to disobey God.

From the time sin separated man from God, man's information about himself and the world he lives in became tainted and twisted (perverted) by his own, self-centered thinking and the influences of that which is satanic or demonic. *(See Romans 1.18–32; 3.10–20, 23; 8.6–8 and Ephesians 2.1–3 for some Scriptural background on this).*

This sinful, fleshly, carnal, and Adamic nature has been passed on through birth to all following generations of men and women. It continues to this present day.

The concept of the Carnal Nature is seen by numerous Bible scholars as having to do with a person who has been spiritually Born-Again but is more influenced by natural fleshly thinking than spiritual thinking. Regardless, to think or act carnally comes from the sin-nature that is a part of the fallen human condition.

The natural-man speaks primarily of a person who has a world-view that is godless at best and outright ungodly at worst. The natural-man is a person who has not come to God through Christ in repentance and faith in the salvation provided through the sacrificial death of Christ on the cross. It is a person who has not been Born-Again.

## REGENERATION: THE NEW CREATION STATE

Therefore, if anyone is in Christ, he is a **new creation**; old things have passed away; behold, all things have become new. *(II Corinthians 5.17 NKJV)*

**SPIRITUAL-NATURE.** Only God can awaken and enlighten the spirit in a person *(John 6.44 & 16.7–15)* to the fact that they are separated from God (this is often referred to as the work of Conviction). This results in the realization that he or she is a sinner and needs the Savior, Who is God's Son, Jesus Christ, so that the person believes and repents, and God does the miraculous work of regeneration in that person called the New Birth, or being Born-Again as spoken of in John 1.12–13; 3.3–21. There are numerous other Scriptures on this as well such as Titus 2.11–14 and 3.3–8 among others.

When Christ becomes our Lord and Savior then there is a new nature birthed in us. That nature is referred to in the Scriptures as the spiritual man, the new man, and the like *(I Corinthians 2.9–14; Galatians 5.16–24; Ephesians 4.17–32, 5.1–20; Colossians 3.1-17).* When we are born-again then our spirit is no longer separated from God in Whom alone there is life. Our spirit has experienced a resurrection or coming to life *(see Ephesians 2.1–10).* We have the Holy Spirit of God dwelling in us to help lead, guide, and teach us about God's Truth that sets us free *(see John 7.37–39; 8.31–36; 14.8–26; 16.12–15; Romans 8.1–17).*

No longer are we stifled by just the tainted, narrow, and limited information coming through the five senses of our physical body and the reasoning of our mind based on just that base information. We now have God's Word of Truth coming through His Spirit working in our spirit. We have the spiritual life of God's written Word *(John 6.63, 68; I Peter 1.22–25)*, as contained in the Bible, that speaks into our spirit resulting in the renewing of our mind which transforms our lives so that we are able to prove what is that good, perfect, and acceptable will of God for our life *(Romans 12.1–2)*.

## THE SATANIC AND THE DEMONIC

Is there a real Devil (also, called Satan and Lucifer)? Jesus stated that there is. The Bible teaches that there is. The world we live in bears abundant and tragic evidence there is.

Satan (or, the devil) is a powerful and evil angelic being *(Job 1.6–12; 2.1–7)* that is set in opposition to all who would live a righteous life. Through pride he rebelled against God *(inferred in Ezekiel 28.15, 17 cf. I Timothy 3.6)*. Satan deceived and enticed man to sin *(Genesis 3.1–24; II Corinthians 11.3; Revelation 12.9, 20.1–3)* and thus brought sin's corrupting consequences of moral darkness, disease, death, and destruction into the world both spiritually as well as physically.

Satan led a host of other angels to join him in his rebellion against God *(inferred in Revelation 12.4; II Peter 2.4; Jude 1.6)*. Jesus said the devil is a liar and murderer *(John 8.43–44 cf. II Corinthians 11.13–15 and Acts 5.3)* and comes like a thief to steal, kill, and destroy *(Matthew 13.24–25, 36–39; Mark 4.15; John 10.10)*. Jesus was sent by His Father to destroy the works of the devil *(I John 3.8; Acts 10.38; Matthew 4.23–24; 8.16)*. Satan has sought to both stop and destroy Christ *(Matthew 4.8–10; John 13.2; Luke 22.2–6)*.

Satan (the devil) is the ultimate principal power and manipulator through his demonic host of all the present world-views and systems that stand in opposition to God and the true knowledge of Him in this world *(Luke 4.5–8; John 12.31, 14.30, 16.11; II Corinthians 4.3–4; Ephesians 6.10–12; I John 5.19; Revelation 12.9–12, 16.12–14, 18.1–2)*.

Satan (the devil) is NOT a negative all-powerful and all-present god. He is a fallen angel that can only be in one place at one time. Even so, his influence can be felt throughout the world by means of the fallen angels, and/or, demons that follow him who vary in power. This means, although evil is present and experienced everywhere, there are and will be specific places in the world where powerful Satanic and demonic strongholds exist in which evil is much stronger and more destructive than in other places whether nations, governments, religion, cities, areas, groups, or individuals.

**DEMONS AND THE DEMONIC.** Predominantly in the New Testament demons are clearly seen as corrupt, evil, and malicious spirits that can and do inflict severe disorders, pain, sicknesses, and the like on mankind physically, spiritually, and mentally *(e.g., Matthew 12.43-45, 15.22–28; Mark 5.1–20; 9.14–29; Luke13.10–17)*.

> *NOTE: I am not saying nor does the Bible teach that all sickness, pain, disorders, and the like are caused by demon spirits versus bacteria, viruses, physical imbalances, genetic disorders, accidents, and the like. "Now Jesus went about...healing all kinds of sickness and all kinds of disease among the people...and those who were demon possessed, epileptics, and paralytics; and he healed them all" (Matthew 4.23-24 NKJV). I have underlined certain words to emphasize the variety and differences in afflictions even though, at times, there may be similarities (just as there is between viral and bacterial pneumonia).*

It appears that just as individual men or women have their own personalities, special abilities, and the like so it is with demons *(Luke 11.26; Mark 9.29 "this kind")*. These corrupt and malicious spirits hate God and all that God has created.

In reading the Gospels of Matthew, Mark, and Luke in the New Testament it is readily seen that one of Jesus' major aspects of ministry was casting out demons during His earthly ministry. During Jesus' earthly ministry He empowered the 12 disciples and then 70 others with power over demonic spirits *(Luke 9.1 and 10.17)*. The early church in the book of Acts continued in this aspect of the Lord's ministry after Jesus' death, resurrection, ascension, and the outpouring of the Holy Spirit *(Acts 5.3, 7-9, 13.8–12, 16.16--19, 19.11–20)*.

There are no actual statements in the Scriptures telling us where these evil spirits originated from—only that they exist and are present in this world. Numerous Bible scholars believe demons could possibly be the fallen angels that followed Satan in his rebellion against God.

Satan (called Beelzebub in Matthew 10 and Mark 3) is said to be the ruler over the demons which would make them his emissaries, or messengers and ministers *(Mark 3.22–26)*. Both Satan and his angelic/demon spirits will all be cast into Hell after Jesus' return to earth *(Matthew 25.41; Revelation 20.1–3, 10)*.

Anyone who reads through the Bible will see that Satan (the devil), his fallen angelic following, and/or demons are real and never to be taken lightly. They are ultimately among the most deadly enemies of humanity and especially any who would earnestly serve our Lord Jesus Christ *(Ephesians 6.10-18; I Peter 5.8–9)*. The clearest revelations about Satan, the fallen angels, and demons are found in the New Testament—as is true of all major Biblical doctrines and subjects.

Some of the darkest hours of evil manifested throughout human history on both a world-wide or national scale as well as in local communities have come as a result of Satan and the demonic. There is, without question, very deep, deep evil in our world that goes far beyond just human mental disorders, body chemistry imbalance, behavior shaped by bad living conditions of abuse, poverty, violence, neglect, hate, and the like as an explanation.

There are more Scripture references to both Satan and other evil angelic beings along with evil demonic spirits than I have given in this brief article. A reading through of the Bible (especially the New Testament) will give you a volume of references and insight as to what is being spoken of here.

As I have shown you in a few of many Scripture references, Jesus confronted Satan himself along with his demonic host throughout his ministry.

As previously mentioned, the Church in the Book of Acts had to deal with these malicious spirits. There are ongoing references in the epistles (letters to the churches and individuals) of how these evil spirits hindered the ministers of the early church plus there are prophetic statements made concerning Satan and demons and the part they will have in the end times.

And then in the last book of the Bible, the Book of Revelation, you find them raging in battle against Christ and His Church as they meet their final doom that they already knew was coming *(Matthew 8.29)*.

# ACKNOWLEDGEMENTS

First and foremost I thank God for His immeasurable love and grace to me in His Son, Jesus Christ. Any part of my life, my ministry, my messages, and my effectiveness for genuine life change in others is all due to His work of life change in and through me. Only what He gives and does makes the eternal differences in any of our lives.

Then I thank God for my wife, Darlene, who has stood so faithfully with me in marriage and ministry since June 1, 1957, when we committed our lives to one another with the sacred oaths of holy matrimony. She has been and remains to this day a great believer and encourager of my ministry including this ever relevant message on *The Dynamics of Forgiveness*. She is a beautiful woman of God who has worked unceasingly at my side with great integrity. She has a great ministry in music and to women given by God that though complimenting my ministry through the years is distinct and stands on its own as well.

And I thank the many men and women of God that our Lord in His divine design and will chooses to impact and bless our lives with. Numerous ones of them have played a role in seeing this book and its message go out over the years. Some key persons who played an important part in the publication of the first book edition, were Everett Smith and Brenda Moore of Northridge, California, and Billy Moore of Bentonville, Arkansas

The second book is now a reality because of a couple like Brock and Bethany Ashurst of our former pastorate at First Assembly of God in El Centro, California, who feel that God put it into their heart to make the update and expansion of this book in its newer form a reality for the many people who will read and be eternally changed by these truths on *The Dynamics of Forgiveness*. I often say, "Things don't just happen; they are made to happen." Thank you Brock and Bethany for helping me fulfill this long time tugging and goal of my heart.

To Susan Stanley, a member of North Central Church in Spring, Texas, where Darlene and I now make our church home, I say from a heart of gratitude thank you for your amazing computer gifts. She was able to take my hand drawn visual aids plus ideas for the *Eye of Forgiveness and Eye of Unforgiveness* along with *The Church—One Versus Many* and transform them into professional quality works suited for printing. Thank you Susan for helping me to illustrate to others what I feel God put into my heart.

I want to send out a very big "thank you" as well to author Dale Van Steenis who read the first book and encouraged me to pursue this updated and enlarged edition; to authors Martha Bolton, Mavis Lewis, Gerald W. Davis and to Bible teacher Joel Fortenberry who took the time to read the developing manuscript of this new and updated edition. Your suggestions, comments, questions, and encouragement were an invaluable help to me.

And I would be amiss if I did not thank Steve Butler who so faithfully worked the electronic side of my radio broadcast, Timely Truth, in Imperial Valley California for my final years in El Centro. He got my original book into a computer form so that the re-write, revision, and updating was made significantly easier. What a blessing and help this was.

And there are numerous others whose lives have been deeply impacted by this forgiveness message who have been involved in encouraging me to update and reprint the book.

To my wife, to all of you who have so blessed my life, and to our Lord I am so grateful and thankful. I believe that there will be many, many others who will be forever changed and set free in their life and walk with the Lord because of you.